Pitman
Education
Library

Out-of-school Activities

Gerald Haigh

Cartoon illustrations
by Larry

Pitman Publishing

First published 1974

Sir Isaac Pitman and Sons Ltd
Pitman House, Parker Street, Kingsway, London WC2B 5PB
PO Box 46038, Banda Street, Nairobi, Kenya

Sir Isaac Pitman (Aust.) Pty Ltd
Pitman House, 158 Bouverie Street, Carlton, Victoria 3053, Australia

Pitman Publishing Corporation
6 East 43rd Street, New York, NY 10017, USA

Sir Isaac Pitman (Canada) Ltd
495 Wellington Street West, Toronto 135, Canada

The Copp Clark Publishing Company
517 Wellington Street West, Toronto 135, Canada

£ 33506
371.89
HA1

Text set in 10/11 pt. IBM Journal, printed by photolithography,
and bound in Great Britain at The Pitman Press, Bath

G.4667/4668:15

To Elizabeth and Ruth,

for putting up with the presence in their play-room

of a quick-tempered dad with a typewriter

Contents

Preface

Any teacher entering the profession today is likely to find himself (or herself — there are many places in this book where the masculine has to stand for both) becoming deeply enough committed to the children in his charge to want to extend his contact with them beyond the confines of the school building and of the school's hours of work.

To a certain extent, indeed, he may not be able to help himself, because so many schools are positively alive with out-of-school activity. If you walk past a large secondary school at 5.30 p.m. you are very likely to find it ablaze with light, brass band music echoing forth, plays being rehearsed behind lighted windows, and busy mechanical sounds issuing from the workshops.

This book purports to do no more than tell what one moderately experienced teacher knows about out-of-school activities. It is not an instruction manual, and the reader will look in vain if he wants to know the rules of basketball or how to make a ski-lift out of egg boxes; for such things he must turn to more specialized volumes.

I have attempted to have a look at voluntary activities, as it were, from the sharp end, to see what the main features are which present themselves to the practising teacher who finds himself supervising them.

I have done this by reviewing, in a very personal way, with very little attempt at dead-pan objectivity, some of the major fields of out-of-school activities as they actually happen, trying all the time to draw out those practical aspects which might not occur to anyone who has had limited experience.

It has seemed to me that I could only do this in a realistic way by confining myself to those activities in which I have myself been directly involved, or at least to those about which I have been able to have discussion with the teachers in charge. For this reason, I do not pretend that every single out-of-school activity is covered. I doubt, in fact, whether it would be possible ever to achieve such a complete coverage of the field, for the multiplicity of voluntary

activities in school is rapidly outstripping any writer's powers of description. Think at random of a hobby, sport or pastime and somewhere in the United Kingdom, you can bet your boots, there will be a school which does it. I am confident that had I looked hard enough I would have found a school which had a taxidermy society or a human cannonball instructional group.

Nevertheless, I feel that this collection of ideas and information will be useful, because the major areas are dealt with, and in any event many of the principles are general ones and can be extended into fields other than the ones directly described.

I have been helped in my search for information by many people, some of whom are listed below, and all of whom have my thanks. Working on this book has brought me the pleasure of making many new acquaintances in the teaching profession.

A particular word of thanks must go to Joseph Newman, a senior colleague, whose experience of schools and of teaching exceeds my own in every way, and who was kind enough to read my typescript at very short notice. Not only did he offer numerous helpful suggestions, but he saved me from the embarrassment of a number of errors both of fact and of grammar.

Any mistakes which remain, and any opinions which are expressed — and there are plenty of those — are, needless to say, all my own!

Thanks then, to: Clive Taylor; John Adams; Bryan Frieze; Tony Bill; John Sutton; David Rimmer; Roger and Sue Thompson; David Cleasby; Paul Clark; David Woodhead.

Bedworth,
Warwickshire.   Gerald Haigh

1
The Reasons Why

It would be as well to start off by trying to define what we mean by "out-of-school activities". This might at one time have been a fairly easy definition to make, when the distinction between school and the outside world was clear. The bell rang, the big wooden door thudded shut and all was silence save for the odd muffled shriek which permeated forth into the outside world.

Now, however, with the liberalization of the curriculum and the dawning realization that education is involved with real life, the boundary is not nearly so clear cut. Children habitually go out of their schools to find out about things, and outsiders more and more commonly come in.

It should be made clear, though, because a number of young teachers and students are not always sure of this, that "out-of-school activities" does not mean lessons outside. An activity which is part of the formal curriculum is normally considered as an "in-school" activity whether it happens in the classroom or in the shadow of Stonehenge.

My own test has been to ask "Is it voluntary?" If a school activity takes place largely out of school hours — whether inside or outside the school building — and is attended by children who have volunteered, then to my mind it is an out-of-school activity. Obviously there is such variety in modern education that this definition is bound to leave some loose ends — there are some schools, after all, at which lesson attendance itself is voluntary — but in general I think that I have written in this book about the sort of things which most teachers would recognize as out-of-school activities.

1

Supply and Demand

Having defined the field, the next step is to see why there has grown up the very rich field of voluntary activities which undoubtedly exists in British schools. Why do children take part? Why are they *urged* to take part? And — a question not often asked — what makes the teachers give their time and energy in amounts which at times seem almost masochistic?

No one ever seems to have doubted that it is good for children to take some interest in school outside of their lessons. Employers of school leavers, and interviewers at places of further and higher education, always seem to like applicants who can show some evidence of having done something besides poring over logarithms and memorizing the details of the Fashoda incident. Teachers too are noticeably — some would say notoriously — likely to be more sympathetic to a shirker or a delinquent if he turns out with the rugby team every Saturday.

The traditional justification has always been that such activities "broaden the mind". No one seems to be sure what this means precisely. It was easier to understand, perhaps, in the past, when schools were full of pinch-faced urchins who had never seen a cow. To take them outside the city boundary was an act as obviously educational and worthwhile as anything which might be done in school.

The young teacher might be forgiven for thinking that the necessity for this sort of mind-broadening is past. Colour television and package tours, after all, have brought the world into the reach of everyone.

It is interesting, however, to test this by asking questions around a class of children. Teachers are often slow to grasp the utter barrenness of the world which many urban children inhabit. A teacher fresh from college and facing a class of secondary school children for the first time might do well to ask them some questions like this:

How many of you have been into the city centre in the past month?
How many of you have ever been on a train?
How many of you know where the local library is?
How many of you know what a book token is?

How many of you have ever *made anything* at home?
You can make up lots of others like this.

Obviously this is a problem which has to be faced by education as a whole, not just by out-of-school activities, but all the same there is a very clear answer for anyone who thinks that the modern child has broader horizons than his forefathers had, and therefore is less in need of help from dedicated teachers who are prepared to give up their time.

In too many cases the world of the urban school child revolves, when he goes out in the evening, around the street corner and local chip shop.

He stands about staring into space and waiting for something exciting to happen, like a slate falling off the roof or a fire in a dustbin. English teachers complain constantly that their children cannot write about anything, because they have never done anything. They lead lives of terrifying emptiness.

The concept of cultural deprivation is now being questioned and it is undeniable that we have often been far too ready to force our middle-class assumptions down the throats of our charges.

Nevertheless it remains true that the homes of many children provide no contact worth speaking of with books, and only limited practice in language. Money is not always the problem here; some of these very children are given expensive record players and foot-ball season tickets as presents. If only they could be taken to the theatre or to see some interesting places instead.

What makes teachers so angry about it all is the apparent failure of society to convert increased prosperity into higher cultural achievement.

It is right that teachers should deplore this situation, but it is important too that they recognize it as a symptom of earlier educational failure.

If the vicious circle is ever to be broken so that future genera-tions can reap some improvement, then teachers should recognize that in many cases, school provides the only contact which a child has with anything remotely artistic or cultural, and that an effort must be made to rise to the challenge which this situation presents.

As there is only a limited amount of time available in school, and as so much of the spare time of our children is in dire need of filling, it follows that a large part of the answer lies in out-of-school activities.

It would be idle to suggest that all teams, clubs and societies in schools are started for high-flown missionary motives, however. Activities are started by individual teachers, and when one of them does so, it is not usually with any overt long-term sociological aim in mind. There are, nearer at hand, practical and worthwhile advantages which accrue to the individual child and which are more likely to be considered.

It is commonly believed, for instance, that a horrible lad who mooches around the school kicking first-formers high into the air and intimidating the caretaker's dog, might well turn to canoe-building or pole-vaulting as a dissolute turns to Salvationism, becoming clean-limbed, pure of mind and diligent in his new found interest.

There are, however, some reservations to be made to this. An interest outside his lessons might well enable a child to have success which eludes him in other fields and he may, as a result, become generally more settled in school. The notion must not be stretched, however, to the point of believing in direct carry over from one to the other. This needs to be said because it is sometimes believed by wishfully thinking teachers that out-of-school activities will solve all sorts of problems which in fact they will not. Success at canoe-building will not necessarily bring about success at mathematics; hard work and co-operation on the athletic field do not automatically mean hard work and co-operation in the classroom, *even when the same teacher is involved in both places.*

This is not to doubt the validity of out-of-school activities. Success outside the classroom can sometimes give a child a stake in the school which he has not been able to establish in any other way, and which might prevent him from going completely off the rails. The particular school brass band of which I have written more than once in this book performs this saving function in the case of more than one of its members. The master in charge has the knack of recruiting some of the wilder members of the establishment and turning their energies to the production of brazen chords rather than to the burning down of the neighbourhood.

A Life-time Interest

It would be satisfying to record that another benefit for the children who stay to join in activities after school lies in the fact that they are equipped to carry on a hobby or interest into adult life. The cold truth, though, is less encouraging. Of all the boys and girls who learn at school to play an instrument, or to make things, only a small fraction carry their interest on after they have left. This is a problem which teachers starting new activities or taking over existing ones would do well to ponder.

It is true that the outlets for hobbies and pastimes are harder to seek in the outside world than they are in school. Adult clubs and societies have to be sought out and their meetings may well take place a long way from the potential member's home, with the prospect of having to turn out in the rain after a day at work. The effort of ferreting out information among strangers, too, is too much for some of our young people. There are grounds, of course, for believing that there is evidence here of failure on our part. We teach our youngsters the skills to go with their interest, but we may well be failing to teach them the confidence and initiative which will enable them to keep up their interests in the outside world.

It is worth thinking, then, of ways in which school children might be encouraged to go on with their activities when they have left school. One way is to hold an out-of-school activity at a time when former pupils can attend, and to encourage them to do so. This has a value all its own — it can only be good for generations to mix in this way. It hardly solves, however, the problem of helping youngsters to cut adrift from the school group and to find its adult counterpart.

More constructive is a deliberate attempt to cultivate links with adult organizations. This might be done by teachers seeking out and writing to the secretaries of their adult counterparts and organizing visits and competitions. It would be good to have big hairy rugby players explaining to a first year pack the correct technique for taking a bite out of the opposing prop's thigh.

The best way of forging such links is to use contacts which already exist. The most usual sort of contact is where a teacher is

himself already involved in an adult organization out of school.
Many local musical directors and dramatic producers are teachers

by profession, for instance, and yet many of them never think of
using their influence to introduce pupils and ex-pupils into their
fields of activity. This is a pity, because it is evident that it can be
done. I recall, for instance, that a number of Guthlaxton School
boys used to sing in the British United Company's Male Voice
Choir in Leicester when their music teacher was its conductor, and
that because of this a number of the boys became very active in
the musical life of the City.

We must try to maximize this sort of thing. A lot of teachers
play rugby and other team games, and there is an obvious opportunity here for them to introduce school leavers into the ranks of
an adult side.

The surface is only just being scratched at the moment. Perhaps with the growth of schools which are purpose built with the intention of playing a leading part in the life of the community, there will be an improvement in the situation.

I do not think that the lack of contact is entirely the fault of teachers. The effort could just as easily come from the other side. With one or two notable exceptions — such as in the brass band world — adult groups do very little in the way of reaching out to schools. Those in charge would do well to think about this, particularly as it is a common complaint among adult groups that they cannot recruit enough young people. Some choral societies appear at first glance to have an average age of ninety-three, several members being visibly propped up by those on either side to prevent their keeling over into the audience.

Another benefit which a child can reap from being involved in an out-of-school activity is that of being placed in a more relaxed relationship with the teacher in charge than he might be in the classroom situation. I will say more of this in the context of the teacher's role in out-of-school activities. Suffice it just now to point out that, particularly in a large school, extra activities may give children the opportunity to work with teachers with whom they would not otherwise normally come into contact.

A very academically minded boy, for instance, may be brought into contact with the woodwork teacher or the head of the remedial department, and may discover, perhaps to his astonishment, that those who purvey these mundane subjects are not necessarily buffoons who cannot be let loose with anything more important.

Such is the degree of specialization in most of our secondary schools that most pupils are a long time in coming to realize that there is nothing so remarkable about a mathematics teacher who plays the oboe, or a physicist who has heard of Milton. At first they look askance at such unnatural goings-on.

Why do they do it?

And what about the teachers? Why do they become involved in out-of-school activities? I knew one man who ran a youth club in school every night of the week. He was out of his house from eight every morning until after closing time in the evening (youth club work gives you a fair thirst). It would be nice to think that he was making a supreme sacrifice for the kids, but in fact in his case the motivation was simply that he was unhappily married, and any extra time away from the family was a welcome bonus.

I am not trying to suggest, of course, that all clubs and teams are run by potential divorcees. It is simply that the motives for a teacher's involvement in extra work are often more complicated than they appear, and that there is some point in discussing them.

There might still be people who think that a teacher's day ends on the dot of four (and twelve weeks' holiday a year, no less!) These critics have a mental picture of him engaged every day in a grim race to beat the kids to the bus stop to be home in time to get out and man petrol pumps or sell investment plans.

Mind you, there are some like that. I taught next to a chap once who used to have his class lined up at the door five minutes before time. He would stand poised, with his hand on the doorknob, concentrating very hard to achieve the ultimate Stirling Moss reaction time between the first micro-second beat of the electric bell and the whipping open of the classroom door. On a good day he could be hitting thirty in second gear down the drive before the ringing had died away.

It could not be said that out-of-school activities played a very large part in his teaching life! If his union had called on him to work to rule it would have been a complete non-event as far as he was concerned. The whole business in assembly of reading out the sports results and presenting cups and trophies and things must have seemed to him to be a manifestation of a strange and shadowy sub-world of which he knew nothing.

I think, risking the wrath of an older generation by saying it, that there were more teachers like this long ago than there are now. We tend to look back on our own schooldays with nostalgia, thinking that there were always blue skies and firm but kindly masters who told us about Moses in the bulrushes and long division. We had our choirs and camps of course, but in my opinion they were the exception rather than the rule and there were always lots of teachers in the bus queue with us at ten past four.

The difference is that in recent years the magnitude and scope of out-of-school activities has increased enormously so that it is no longer the faithful few who give their time and energy to the children beyond the terms of their contract. Rather it is the minority who do not do so.

The young teacher entering school for the first time may well be surprised by the amount of involvement which is expected. Even if he is not leading or organizing, activities such as plays and garden fêtes have a habit of casting a wide net, and the P.E. staff are always on the look-out for helpers. A teacher who does nothing else might well find himself, with only the scantiest knowledge of the rules, in complete charge of the fixture and player-purchasing policy of the under-twelve shinty team.

The expansion of out-of-school activities has been such that involvement in them has come to be regarded as the norm. These days, a teacher who does nothing but teach and then goes home tends to be looked upon critically both by those in authority and by his colleagues, who feel that he is not pulling his weight.

The new entrant to the profession might be dismayed by this attitude, but it is not difficult to see how it has arisen, and to adjust to it. To aspire to professional status presupposes professional standards of involvement, and the nine to four teacher is on thin ground when it comes to claiming the title of professional educator.

The snag is that this trend leads to teachers' involvement being taken for granted. At its worst this can mean advertisements for teaching posts which stipulate taking part in out-of-school activities as one of the conditions of acceptance.

I suppose we can hardly grumble. If we, as a profession, have worked ourselves into a situation where out-of-school commitment is the normal thing, then it is difficult to see how headmasters can be prevented from trying to make sure their staff comes up to the norm.

The pity is that to some extent this pressure on teachers might tend to cloud the altruistic motives of those who organize activities. A teacher who is energetic and does a lot of out-of-school work may lay himself open to the suspicion, or even the accusation, that he is doing so to further his promotion prospects. A picture may come into the minds of his critics of him trotting with forced casualness past the head's study window leading two hundred cross-country runners, or indulging in loud choir practices well within the earshot of all who matter, visualizing the fulsome praise which will appear on his reference when he applies for a deputy headship.

Most of the time this is unjustified. The thought of material reward might be an added spur to the chap who leads children all over the Black Mountains, but it is hardly enough to cause him to start from scratch if the initial interest is not there.

On the other hand, the reasons for dedication to out-of-school activities are rarely to be found in the field of unalloyed altruism. Even the motives which seem unselfish often turn out to be a disguised form of self-indulgence.

It is no good pretending, for instance, that teachers do not enjoy the satisfaction which is to be gained from sharing a favourite activity with their charges. In this they are like parents who wait patiently for their sons and daughters to grow up so that they can be introduced to judo or spear fishing or whatever.

The particular delight which I take in having a day out with my choir — winning a cup perhaps and singing all the way home on the coach — is, make no mistake, a form of self-indulgence.

There are also teachers whose major interest in life lies in a field which can only be introduced as an out-of-school activity. Their teaching day might be a burden to them, impatiently wished away so that the real business — chess, or the orchestra — can begin.

This leads me to the belief that the real reason some teachers find it easier to get on with children in the out-of-school situation than they do in class is not because the children are more interested in the out-of-school activity than they are in lessons, but because *the teacher* is. Children always respond to enthusiasm, and many of us have lost the habit of keenness in the classroom; we find it again only when urging on a cross-country team or waving a baton at a musical group.

It has been said that poor Mallory, the teacher who died with Irvine on Everest, had difficulty in his relationships with his pupils. If so, it seems strange perhaps, that a man of such qualities and courage should have had this trouble. I wonder, though, whether he ever brought his ropes and equipment into the classroom and if he did, what the reaction was. It might be that the climate in which he worked would not allow such frivolity, but it makes an interesting speculation; there ought to be a pointer here to young teachers.

A teacher who is having difficulty with children in the early stages ought to think very seriously about trying to introduce his own particular interest as an out-of-school activity. This is not because it will make all the children magically well behaved, but because it will give them a chance to see him as a human being. Perhaps, more important, it will enable him to preserve his sanity and give him an area of success and satisfaction at a time when such areas might seem few and far between.

A musical colleague of mine ends his afternoon on one day of the week with a mixed group of first year children of very low ability. He is no beginner, but he is a perfectionist and because of this he finds his work with them discouraging and hard.

"How I look forward," he said to me one day, "to my senior recorder group rehearsal after school on that day."

The teacher — particularly a new teacher who finds the work frustrating and full of disappointments — who goes home at four o'clock every day under a black cloud should, as a matter of urgency, become involved in an activity after school which will allow him the opportunity to make up for some of the troubles of the day.

For most teachers, then, out-of-school activities are by no means a time-consuming chore undertaken out of a sense of duty. There may well be times when he wonders why he was fool enough to get involved. For some this point comes on a snowy Saturday morning when the rugby team has turned up four men short. For me it usually happens about a week before an important choir occasion when I am fighting a losing battle to gather people together for rehearsals.

In the end, though, we have to admit that we enjoy ourselves immensely. There is a lot of satisfaction to be gained from working with children in a relaxed and friendly atmosphere untrammelled by the demands of a syllabus or of examination requirements.

2
Sports and Games

Of all out-of-school activities it is probably sport which holds the firmest and most time-honoured place. The football match which is so important in *Tom Brown's Schooldays* was strictly speaking an out-of-school activity, and every old-established school will have a collection of sports team photographs dating back to the time when the players sported kneebreeches and moustaches. The photographs of the school orchestra and of wild-eyed lads playing Hamlet tend to bear much more recent dates.

The principle of voluntary participation by staff and pupils, which is a feature of most out-of-school activities, takes its biggest knock in the field of sport. It is accepted without question that the physical education staff of a secondary school will run sports teams which train and play their fixtures outside school hours. They will normally call upon other members of staff to help but, even so, the average P.E. teacher is busy most evenings, most lunchtimes and every Saturday morning.

Not that they ever complain, mind you. Most of them are gluttons for punishment in fact. Only recently I attended an evening cross-country match, and as I walked to the start I overheard two track-suited masters animatedly discussing the possibility of starting an inter-school gymnastics competition which was sure to take up another couple of evenings a week. P.E. teachers are so energetic as a rule that it makes you tired just to watch them. It is not that they are celibate or abstemious of habit either, my goodness, but that is another story!

It probably helps that a lot of P.E. teachers come from a background where they themselves have been accustomed to training and competing in various sporting activities in their spare time.

The ranks of good class athletics and rugby football are well sprinkled with teachers and student teachers.

Many of these physical educationists also admit to being more interested in sports coaching than they are in the day to day business of class gymnasium work, and the main outlet for their interest is likely to be outside the school timetable.

But whatever the reasons, as far as out-of-school activities are concerned, the P.E. and games teachers are really conscripts — albeit willing ones.

It is these people that the young teacher will be assisting if he is not a P.E. specialist and yet volunteers or is coaxed or bribed into helping with games in his spare time. Their dedication very often proves difficult to live up to, and it should be remembered that a teacher who does agree to help out with games is letting himself in for a fair degree of work and responsibility. The usual thing is that the volunteer is given one of the teams to look after. This sounds all very well to the young man who is a soccer enthusiast and is given the under fourteen eleven to mould as he likes, but he should be aware of the snags before he starts.

For one thing, there is the difficulty of fielding a full team for every fixture. The principle is held in most schools that if a child is picked to play or to run for the school then his participation is compulsory. The successful enforcement of this idea in the teeth of waning enthusiasm on the part of the boys and girls and their parents is a continual thorn in the side of games masters and mistresses, and of the head teachers who seek to encourage and support them.

The teacher who volunteers to go off on a Saturday with the intermediate cross-country team, for example, is quite likely to find something of this sort.

Of the twelve who are picked, six will be standing at the appointed meeting place in good time (albeit with only five pairs of running shoes between them). Sometimes, and this is a rare delight, a couple of enthusiastic dads will be there as well. Of the other six, three will turn up more or less on time (with one pair of shoes between them). The remaining three will be totally unwilling, although one may come along at the last minute (without shoes), his nerve having failed him.

The coach will wait fifteen minutes, with the master in charge pacing up and down gazing into the distance. If the missing ones live near enough, he may go and drag them out, but the chances are that the coach will eventually leave with two short.

The following Monday the teacher has to decide what to do about the ones who failed to arrive. It is certain the the young teacher who has this problem should not carry it alone, but should seek the advice of the master in charge of P.E. There may well be some investigation and ultimately some punishment to be meted out, but the legal issue involved in punishing children for not turning out to a voluntary activity is frankly a bit tricky, and the responsibility should be taken by someone in authority.

That punishment is used in these circumstances is an indication of the frustration that is suffered by those who try to give young-sters experience of competitive sport outside school hours. The task becomes more difficult every year, but in most cases the fight goes on because there are still enough youngsters who are interest-ed to make it worth trying to do something to encourage the support of the apathetic.

It soon becomes wearing, though, and a young teacher brought up in the middle-class conventions of loyalty to the team, and the honour of selection, is easily nonplussed by having to listen to a boy who did not turn out on Saturday "because I had to go out with my dad". The situation is even worse on the girls' side because of the problem of the Saturday job. In many towns the lady games teachers have given up the struggle of trying to run Saturday fixtures.

Perhaps the only really satisfactory way for the young teacher to avoid these difficulties with his own team, is not by threats of punishment, but by his own enthusiasm. If he holds regular and interesting team practice sessions, so that his team members come to know each other and to know him, and if he demonstrates his own commitment to these sessions by taking the trouble to change properly for them and by throwing himself in with visible zeal — even when he was in the "Dolce Vita" only five hours before — then he will reap more benefit than he would by trying to crack the whip over a sullen bunch of youngsters.

It is particularly important — and this rule will be repeated elsewhere, for it is a cardinal one of out-of-school activities — that a training session or practice must never be cancelled except in the direst circumstances. Once children have the idea that "Sir" only holds the weekly coaching session when it suits him, then they will begin to attend when it suits *them* — and they can hardly be blamed.

On top of these general comments, here are a few thoughts about particular sports and games.

Association Football

Given the choice, this is what most boys will play. In schools where rugby is the rule, the boys will often form unofficial soccer teams or will play for outside organizations. School football in England is very highly organized under the overall auspices of the Football Association and there is a full programme of league and cup competitions in every part of the country. Any teacher who finds himself in charge of a school football team without knowing much about it can do no better than to contact the local Schools' F.A. Secretary — such is the ubiquitous nature of the game that no school is far away from one of these gentlemen, who are all hard-working schoolmasters themselves. From this source all sorts of help in the way of coaching schemes and the sort of fixtures which are available can be obtained.

Many teachers and officials in schoolboy soccer are becoming worried, incidentally, about the appearance in the game at their level of some of the more ridiculous aspects of professional play. It is a sad sight to see eleven-year-old lads kissing one another after a score, or appealing violently to "The Ref", who is no doubt their teacher but has lost this status as far as the young players are concerned by picking up the whistle.

A teacher faced with this must be quite ruthless. The sad part about the professional game is that the result transcends all else, and so dirty play is condoned by managers, and players of genius are allowed to get away with murder because of their ability to score goals. A team of youngsters may assume that both these criteria will hold good for them, and they must be shown in no uncertain terms that this is not so. From the outset, the players must be told of the code of conduct which is expected, and that anyone who breaks this will be dropped — or even pulled off the field on the spot. Having made the threat, it must then be carried out, right to the point of dropping four or five badly needed

players on the eve of a big match. The message will soon seep through. I knew a young all-England forward who was dropped from his humble house team for rolling his eyes at a referee's decision. It did him no end of good.

Some teachers and heads have become so concerned about all this that they have rejected the game altogether in favour of rugby.

Young teachers are often called upon to referee in situations where they would rather not — mainly because they are not sure of the rules. (This is not just a soccer situation, of course.) There is only one way out, and that is to decide on the rules you are going to play to, and stick to them through thick and thin. The problem is not so much the players as the "experts" on the touchline.

Perhaps a lesson in how to deal with them can be learned from a friend of mine who stopped a game one Saturday and walked to a group of groaning dads. He explained in fairly brisk terms that he was doing the job voluntarily, and that if one of them would prefer to take over, this would be perfectly acceptable. No one was keen on this idea, and for the rest of the match they were less forthcoming with their catcalls.

Rugby Union Football

A lot of teachers have played and still play rugby, and are anxious to see the tradition carried on in their schools. If the area is predominantly soccer minded, this can cause a rather artificial situation with the game having little or no foothold in the grass roots (if you will forgive the mixed metaphor).

The teacher who becomes involved will find that there are a number of disadvantages to rugger. One is that it requires more players than most other games, and so the problem of finding a team every week is that much more difficult. It is also true that the skills are difficult for small boys to master — the game does not "miniaturize" easily because it is essentially a game of power and strength. To illustrate what I mean, I recall that tragi-comic experience of seeing a twelve-year-old boy take the ball from what was passing as a ruck, gaze purposefully at the posts and essay a drop goal from thirty yards. In fact, he would have been hard pressed to kick the ball over a greenhouse from ten feet!

There was also the case of the winger who had to stop for a breather during a heroic seventy-yard dash for the line.

Still, it is a good game played by the right sort of boys — and that means the big ones. There is a good case for sticking to soccer until the fifth or sixth form is reached The boys would probably then enjoy both games better, because soccer is usually their preference when they are younger and rugger would be more acceptable to them as something of a change after four or five years in school. The skills would come very quickly to the ones who had the aptitude.

Rugby League

This is the professional game. At the senior level it came into being on the sole issue of professionalism, and professionalism is the reason for its continuing existence. It is, however, played in parts of the north by schoolboys, and as they are obviously amateurs we are treated to the spectacle of Amateur Rugby League, which is something that only a bunch of teachers could have thought up.

Cross-country Running

I do not think that many boys actually enjoy this, although an awful lot of them seem to do it. The start of the national championships, for instance, looks very much like the scene outside a large car factory three seconds after clocking off time.

Their reasons for competing may have something to do with masochism, or sludge fetishism perhaps. Certainly if you stand at the finish of a race and watch the team managers trying to scrape enough mud off their runners to read the numbers on their backs, you will be hard put to offer any explanation at all.

A pointer to any teacher who takes over a team, or who starts one, is that the sport is considerably more interesting and enjoyable over an actual countryside course. This is difficult, as most schools are obviously surrounded by houses and roads. It is worth trying, however, and a bit of work with a large-scale map and some ground work is called for. It might even be feasible to organize a course outside the town and to transport the team to the start. If the course is a really good one, with woodland and ploughed fields and a good feeling of remoteness, then the added trouble will be worth it. The need for careful negotiation with landowners and farmers is obvious — cross-country running is hard enough without the added burden of a backside full of lead shot.

It can be done, though. King Henry VIII school in the heart of Coventry has a course outside the town with real ploughland and woods.

It was in Coventry, too, that I learned another tip which might be applicable in some other places. I was at a race at one of the comprehensive schools in that town. When the runners were lined up, everyone waited for the resident P.E. master to give them the usual instructions about the course. This is a procedure which usually takes several minutes and requires the aid of a blackboard map apparently drawn in purple chalk by a play school group. While it is going on, the runners leap about in an ineffectual attempt to stave off frostbite, taking not the slightest bit of notice.

In this particular case, though, the master strolled out to the front, pointed to the ground and said:

"See this white line lads? Follow it!"

It appeared that he had been all round the course with a white line marker.

Even with this sort of help, the course will need to be marked by boys standing at regular intervals with flags. Road crossings are particularly difficult, and should invariably be manned by teachers. Those of us who have done this sort of thing would be grateful if organizers would remember to let us know when the events are all over. It is no fun to stand about in the freezing cold for hours wondering if it is safe to go home or whether there is another race still to come.

Cricket

The disadvantages of playing competitive cricket at school are so enormous that it would probably have died out long ago were it not for the fact that teachers feel a moral responsibility to keep alive a game which is so firmly interwoven into our national culture.

It goes on a long time, is very vulnerable to the weather, and the shortness of the school summer term is a ruinous influence. A school which completes ten fixtures in a season in any one age group can count itself fortunate. The growing strength of school athletics is another factor which menaces cricket.

All this is a great pity, and teachers should throw off all temptation to give the game up in favour of softball, and do their level best to keep it going. Its overwhelming quality is the unique way it can teach players to combine an aggressive competitive spirit with gentlemanly conduct. Not many games, to say the least, can do this.

One word of warning to the teacher who goes off with a cricket team. Have a careful look at the wicket. Looking after a wicket is a skilled job, and few school groundsmen have the time to do it

properly. As a result a lot of school wickets are simply too dangerous to play on. If you have any doubts, make every teacher in
sight aware of your doubts so that even if you give way on the
grounds of inexperience, you will have shaken off some of the
responsibility. A teacher who really knows his cricket and is confident of the unfitness of a wicket should not allow lowly status
in the profession to stop him from taking his team home again.
After all, cricket played on an unfit surface is not only dangerous,
it is a bad game of cricket.

Athletics

One of the most agreeable things about school athletics is the mixing of the sexes which it brings about. An inter-school match
involving mixed schools will normally be played out between both
boys' teams and girls' teams, and for a short time their almost
totally separate sporting worlds are brought together.

One of the sad things, on the other hand, is the fact that standards have become so high in school athletics that if a child is to
reach the top and represent his county or even his country, he
generally needs more training and coaching than most schools are
able to provide. As a result, county and national championships
are more and more dominated by youngsters who are to all intents
and purposes club athletes who wear their school colours for the
day.

A teacher who has such an athlete in his care — either as a
member of a team or simply as a member of a class or a tutorial
group — would do well to keep a careful eye on the demands
which his club makes upon him. Some athletic clubs — and other
sorts of sporting clubs for that matter — show too little sense of
responsibility towards the development of the child as a whole. If
the pressures seem to be too great, so that the child begins to
worry or to perform badly in his school work, then the head of
the school and the child's parents should be advised.

A teacher coming into a school and trying to find a niche in an
already fairly well organized athletics programme could do no
better than apply himself to the coaching of throwing events.

They are all too often neglected and this is something that is reflected by the generally dismal performance of British throwers in adult international competition. At school athletics meetings it is far too common to see youngsters desultorily putting the shot and throwing the discus in all sorts of miserable and frankly illegal styles, and you can go to such meetings for years without ever seeing a hammer event.

Youngsters every year seem to be bigger and stronger, and it would be a service to British sport if teachers were able to interest some of these gigantic seventeen-year-old second row forwards of both sexes in the "heavy" events. Here is a ready made wide open field for the young teacher. The coaching techniques can be learned fairly easily and pleasantly in the course of a fortnight at one of the Amateur Athletics Association's Summer Schools.

Hockey

A young man who can play hockey and who goes to teach in an area where it is not usually played by boys has a golden opportunity which he should not fail to sieze. The game usually catches on very quickly, especially among the younger age group in secondary schools — there are a lot of boys who are relieved of the chance to escape from the domination of the young lions of the second form soccer scene.

Older students can often be tempted by mixed hockey, and even the ones who have grown blasé about the whole sporting scene can become mad keen overnight. Girls who for years have done nothing more energetic than wiggling their hips at a discotheque will often take to mixed hockey, which they seem to look upon as a more active version of standing on the street corner with the lads.

Netball

Only one plea here, and that is to young teachers who want to replace it with girls' basketball. Netball has an elegance all its own, and a lot of the skills are just not present in basketball. More important, there are a lot of girls who will love netball but will hate basketball, which is much more boisterous and extrovert in nature.

Swimming

The main difficulty here is the same as in athletics. The degree of commitment which is required from a young swimmer who aims at competitive success is worrying to a teacher who is concerned with the all-round development of the child.

The swimming teacher — as opposed to the out and out swimming coach — must also reconcile the two places which swimming occupies in school life. On the one hand there is the business of teaching all the children to swim so that they can enjoy their holidays that much better and perchance preserve their lives if they are ever swept out to sea on a rubber duck. On the other hand there is the business of swimming as a competitive sport.

A teacher should be in no doubt whatsoever about which of these deserves priority, and it may well be that the only way to preserve conscience is to eschew the coaching of swimming teams altogether and to concentrate on teaching the basics to as many children as possible.

Swimming baths can usually be booked for lunchtime sessions and after school — a call to the baths manager will produce the required information. In dealing with swimming baths' officials — and any other people in that sort of position — it is best to speak to the highest ranking person available. The lower echelons, being usually underpaid, are invariably made up of people who know nothing or, much worse, "know" all sorts of things which are absolutely wrong.

Other Games

Non-specialist teachers who want to become involved in sports and games out of school would do well to explore some of the minor games, which may well lie outside the knowledge or the interest of the P.E. staff. Some of them are easy to organize, requiring little in the way of specialized equipment, and often score with the children simply, because they are different and give a chance to the ones who have felt cut off from the major games because of lack of skill.

Volleyball is a good example. It requires little space and not much equipment, and it involves a fair number of children. Its

introduction into the Olympics and subsequent featuring on television and in educational films about the Games has done a lot to popularize it. Best of all, the range of skill, as it were, is almost limitless. At one end of the spectrum it can be played by people whose co-ordination — or lack of it — would make them look fools with a bat in their hands, and at the other extreme there is every opportunity to demonstrate superb athleticism and tactical skill. Boys and girls love it and it is one of those games which seniors will play for the sheer fun and novelty of it when they would not be seen dead in a rugby shirt.

Softball is also easy to run, but should be treated with caution in the out-of-school context because it might seduce boys from cricket, which is not a good idea at all. (I found the rules of the game and the layout of the pitch in, of all places, the "Encyclopaedia Britannica". If you are stuck, most games are in there.)

Safety and Security

The young teacher who becomes involved in the general supervision of out-of-school sport would do well to remember one or two general points.

Changing-room security is easily overlooked. In an inter-school match or tournament, with lots of children using a changing room, it is particularly important to guard against the possibility of pilfering, with all the subsequent suspicion and embarrassment. The best way is to have a teacher in the changing-room when the children are there whose specific duty is to look after security. When the game is actually in progress it can be locked. (The holder of the key should be easily available in case anyone has to go back during the course of the event, in which case he should be accompanied.) Changing-room pilfering at large inter-school matches is *very* common, and precautions are well worth a great deal of care.

A teacher who accompanies a team to any away fixture should stay with them and make sure they are not an inconvenience to the host staff. To deliver the boys to the gate and then scarper to the pub, for instance, is gross discourtesy. Even worse is to send children unaccompanied, and rely on the kindness of the staff at the other end to look after them.

At any important sports meeting there will be P.E. teachers present, and they usually know a bit about first-aid. Any non-specialist teacher who habitually supervises sports teams should learn some rudimentary first-aid.

In any case of injury which causes doubt — and the "doubt threshold" should be very low indeed — the injured child must be taken home or to the nearest casualty department. Remember though that the parents must be informed, for apart from reasons of common humanity, there is not much that a doctor can do without the consent of the child's parents. Hospitals are *never* annoyed about being worried with injuries which turn out to be trivial.

A child who is unconscious, in great pain or has any of his bits and pieces obviously misshapen needs an ambulance. The time spent waiting for it to arrive is better spent working out how to get it right on to the field than in panicking about with smelling salts and buckets of water.

It follows from this that a teacher who supervises out-of-school sport needs to know the location of the nearest telephone and of the nearest hospital with a casualty department. What the children tell you may not be reliable. Some hospitals, particularly specialist ones, do not have provision for casualties. The local maternity hospital, for instance, will not thank you for rushing in with a stricken footballer across your shoulders like a shot moose!

3
Music

Classroom music teaching is an enormously difficult task. It is in the music room that the clash of the two cultures is at its most clangorous, with the artistic and musicianly teacher swimming hard to keep himself and his classes from being drowned in a sea of tasteless and all-pervading pop.

The trouble is that a child's response to music is a part of his total cultural response. He enjoys pop and ridicules Mozart not because of a conscious judgment, but because of the dictates of the cultural environment he inhabits. If the purveyors of pop culture told him to enjoy Bach, then he would be happy to chant the "Goldberg Variations" on the football terraces. Teachers are a puny force indeed pitted against the giant commercial interests which dominate popular music.

It is perhaps because of all this that many school music teachers turn with relief to their out-of-school musical activities, where they can spend at least some of their time with boys and girls who have an interest in, and some talent for, what they are doing.

After-school music-making also offers an opportunity for the teacher who is an amateur musician rather than a classroom music specialist, and the teacher who has something to offer in this respect will be welcomed with open arms by any school music department.

Some schools have a surprising depth of talent in this direction, and as some indication I give here a list of musical staff in one comprehensive school with seventy teachers. The staffroom contains: a young lady history specialist who conducts a recorder group and sings in the staff—student choir; a maths specialist who takes another recorder group; a remedial teacher who conducts

the staff—student choir; another remedial teacher who conducts
the brass band; a careers teacher who gives piano lessons and helps
with piano playing generally; a chemistry master and a maths
mistress who play violin in the orchestra; about sixteen others who
sing in the staff—student choir.

Any teacher entering a school for the first time should not hide
for long any musical talent which he has, no matter how mean or
lowly it seems to be to him. Even if it means no more than playing
alongside pupil beginners, this is a very valuable contribution and
a tremendous encouragement to the children. It is also a very good
way for the teacher to lose some of the tensions which he might
gather during the day, and to meet pleasant children in a pleasant
setting. (Musical children are always nice — how could they be anything else?)

Musical activity in schools takes a number of forms, and I
propose at this point to take a few of them one at a time.

The Orchestra

This is the fundamental and also the ultimate unit of all music-
making, and so it must be every music teacher's dream to have an
orchestra.

One problem is the expense. It costs something like £3,000 to
equip a school orchestra from scratch with new instruments. This
is clearly prohibitive and a teacher who is building an orchestra
must look for other ways of doing it. Used instruments can be
bought, with specialist advice — even a trained music teacher who
is not a violinist needs a violinist's advice when buying an instrument. The peripatetic staff or someone from the music organizer's
department will help. Or children can be encouraged to buy their
own instruments, with the help of savings schemes and discounts
negotiated with friendly shops.

There has to be money-raising, though. One school had the
chance to buy some tympani which had been declared obsolete
by the local symphony orchestra. They were bought by means
of a loan from the school fund, and were then exhibited at
concerts with notices placed on them inviting contributions. The
fact that they were there on view made the money raising much

easier, and this sort of action should be urged upon the keeper of the school fund if at all possible. Apart from anything else, it makes it easier to snap up bargains.

The music organizer or adviser will often help with instruments. He is much more ready to do so when he sees real evidence of children thirsting to play and of teachers qualified to teach them. He will also help more readily if the school is helping itself. One

adviser told a school: "You buy one cello and I will give you another."

It follows that the organizer must be cultivated by invitations to visit the musical activities of the school, and that the Head must be carefully primed about which levers to pull when he is entertaining him to sherry.

The other difficulty is that of keeping the school orchestra staffed with competent players. Orchestral instruments are difficult to learn, and call for many hours of dedicated practice. Too few children can stand up to this sort of thing. It may be that in our well meant anxiety to take the terror out of education, we have done our children the disservice of hiding from them that there are fields of life where progress is only made by hours of concentrated effort.

Every teacher who runs a school orchestra has stories to tell of boys and girls who have shown keenness to start an instrument, and who have been helped and given the loan of one, only to come along one day with the news that they intend to give it up. The most depressing thing about this is the way their parents allow them to get away with it. Certainly any teacher who experiences this should write to the parents, setting out in detail all the things which have been done to help the child, and pointing out the difficulties caused by what on the surface might seem to be a casual decision.

A teacher who is involved with instrumentalists in school should find out whether the music organizer runs, as many do, an orchestra made up of the better players from the schools which come under his wing. There may well be more than one group, with a structure whereby players can be promoted from one to another. A music teacher who has only one or two good players in his school finds this especially valuable, as it provides a needed outlet for their abilities. He needs to take care that the young musicians he sends are of a calibre to stay the course — and this is a matter of personality rather than of talent. A school can easily fall into disrepute by sending along players who are unreliable in attendance, or who drop out for vague reasons.

Brass Bands

There is a very healthy and thriving brass band movement in schools. This is partly because the instruments are easier to play in the early stages than are many orchestral instruments. The sheer noise and blatant virility of a brass band also appeals to youngsters more than the greater subtlety of an orchestra. They will take the utmost delight in producing ear-shattering sounds that render life as we know it impossible within a radius of half a mile.

There is also a very strong competitive side to brass banding, and a band of almost any standard, right down to the novice level can usually find a competition which will give them a good day out in the company of other enthusiasts, and perhaps the satisfaction of winning a trophy.

The band which I know best thrives in a school which is in a not very culture-conscious catchment area, and in which other musical groups have a constant struggle to keep going. Apart from the appeal of the brass band itself, there are other reasons for this success which the organizer of any sort of group would do well to take to heart.

The teacher who runs the band is single-minded in his enthusiasm. All his rehearsals start on time, and they are never cancelled. The music is always sorted out and ready to play from, and the conductor always arrives knowing exactly what he is going to do. He expects the same sort of relentless dedication from his players, and by and large he achieves it. A peripatetic teacher gives lessons to budding players in the lower part of the school, and these youngsters are enrolled in a junior band knowing that their ultimate aim is to join the senior group, and that to do so is no mean honour.

It is my experience that adult bands are very ready to help youngsters, and a teacher who is interested would do well to go and have a talk to the committee of the local brass band with a view to finding out ways of making contact — pointing out, of course, that the adult band may stand to gain, especially in terms of potential recruits from school-leavers.

Recorders

Since the recorder was revived as part of the rebirth of interest in early music at the beginning of this century, it has become an enormously popular instrument in school, partly because it has the advantage of being inexpensive.

There are disadvantages to this popularity. For one thing, the assumption has grown up that the recorder is just an easy instrument for children. In its turn, this has given rise to a vast amount of bad playing. You can meet many adults who profess to hate the recorder simply because they spent their childhood playing it badly and assumed that this was the only sort of sound it could produce.

As an example, a young colleague of mine once expressed total incredulity on being told that a certain composer was "Professor of Recorder" at a foreign Conservatoire. To her, this seemed on a par with finding out that someone was holder of a Chair of Concertina Playing, or was Reader in Kazoo and Jews Harp at a Musical Academy.

The first priority for a teacher who is asked to take a recorder group, and who is unsure of his own standards, is to come into contact with some *real* recorder playing and if necessary take some lessons of his own. Local schools of music are probably the best source for this, and there is a Society of Recorder Players, with a regional organization.

One recorder enthusiast in the Midlands, who is the head of a music department, keeps up interest and standards among his staff and pupils by occasionally inviting professional musicians who are sympathetic to the recorder to visit the school. This is clearly something which any teacher could do, but fees might be a problem if there is no friendly contact to be exploited. Cultivation of such contacts at musical events and festivals and at residential courses is obviously one way of tackling this.

The teacher in question recently had, for instance, a "Walter Bergmann" day, when Doctor Bergmann came and rehearsed the school's recorder groups and later conducted a concert which included some of his own works. The children gave up a Saturday for this, and gained in return a great deal of enjoyment and the satisfaction of being treated as fellow musicians by a working professional.

Choirs

Whether or not a school is likely to have a flourishing choir depends at least partly upon the region of the country in which the school is situated. I spoke to a teacher from South Wales about this. He was a man after my own heart in that he believed the "Land of Song" thing to be a myth, fostered by the makers of second feature films about colliery disasters, but he did admit that in schools in his part of the world it was not very difficult to recruit boys and girls into choirs.

The same is true in certain parts of Yorkshire and Leicestershire, and there may well be other places where singing is one of the done things.

The main problem about running a choir in a mixed school is that of persuading the boys to take part. For some reason they

find the idea a little unmanly. There are various ways of trying to tackle this. It is possible, for example, to arrange concerts by visiting choirs of hairy miners or barrel chested policemen. Boys will sometimes sing as a male voice group apart from the girls, and then perhaps be seduced into joining the mixed choir. I can offer no real advice, however. The teacher who solves this problem had better write and tell me about it.

The interesting thing is that boys in a boys' school will sing. A case in point is that of a venerable boys' grammar school in a

Midlands city. The school had an able choir, and on one occasion the choirmaster sought to extend his activities by joining forces with the choir from the girls' school across the road. As soon as he did this, the attendance at his own choir dropped, and he was obliged to withdraw from the tainting influence.

"It's a bit like sex," my headmaster said when I was discussing this with him. "You have to do it to know what it's really like."

One way out is to run a mixed choir for staff and pupils. A choir of this sort can achieve a very high standard indeed, because the combination of adult experience and youthful freshness of tone is well nigh unbeatable.

This is being recognized in a negative sort of way by a number of competitive festival committees who, subject to the pressure of die-hard local choral societies, are beginning to exclude choirs which have more than a certain percentage of under eighteens. This is about as short-sighted as you can get from the point of view of the long-term survival of choral singing in this country.

A choir of staff and pupils mixes the two sides together in a way which is of great benefit to them both. Children enjoy being treated like adults by the choirmaster, and delight in the spectacle of their feared maths teacher being bawled out for singing a wrong note. The youngsters also learn a great deal from the adults about such things as confidence and platform manner.

For their part, the staff are often reminded, rather depressingly, of the rate at which young minds can assimilate new material. It is rather disconcerting for a teacher to see a girl reading a comic while she waits for the adults to catch up with learning the notes of a song.

Teachers who are new to choral conducting in school should learn never to under-estimate the abilities of their children. They must be taught to *sing*, not to shout like the chorus of a Lionel Bart musical and, as soon as possible, some part-singing should be attempted. Remember that beginners find it difficult when making early attempts at part-singing to start with each part on a different note. It is usually only the work of a few moments to modify the beginning of a part-song so that it starts in unison and then moves apart, and a simple alteration like this can often make all the difference to the ease with which a novice choir performs a song.

Concerts

Music is intended to be a shared experience, and any teacher who
wants to keep the interest of his musical groups will feel the need
to put on a concert sooner or later. When this urge overcomes a
teacher for the first time, there are one or two things to be kept
in mind.

In the first place, it is important to resist the temptation to put
on groups which are not yet ready to appear in public. It is unfair
to inflict upon an audience a full programme of such agonizing
ineptitude that even the fondest relatives in the audience find their
patience stretched to the uttermost. The unfairness is not only
directed at the suffering audience, of course. It is not reasonable
that the children should be made to think they are doing something delightful to the ear, when it is quite patent that they are
not.

Secondly, whatever the standard of the performers, everyone
will be very grateful if the concert is not too long. Music teachers
can easily become carried away in their programme building, and
audiences have been known to spend many a miserable hour
shuffling their bottoms on those excruciating canvas chairs simply
because the organizer of the concert could not bear to leave anything out.

The third and last little axe which I will hone here is that of
performance.

Young players and singers should be taught and shown by
example that there is more to the business of public music-
making than just shambling up on to the stage, playing a piece
through, and shambling off again before the applause has finished,
avoiding the eye of the audience.

It is necessary to ensure that in any concert the performers are
arranged presentably in the hall, that such things as flowers and
decorations are attended to, and that everyone knows when to
stand up and how to take a bow. It isn't a bad thing either if the
teachers who are conducting or otherwise occupying positions of
prominence wear evening dress. Children should learn about performance and platform manner in their lessons and rehearsals, but
in concerts they should have the opportunity to put them into
practice.

4
The School Play

There cannot be many schools which do not put on some sort of play at least once during the year. This is quite a natural thing, of course, because drama is an activity particularly well suited to the energies and imagination of children. Add to this the fact that sooner or later drama requires an audience, and the school play automatically follows.

This is not to say that all school plays are the same. Self evidently they are not. They vary in scope, presentation and, let it be said, in standard of performance. Of this last, I would say that all that has already been said about standards of performance in musical concerts is equally true of dramatic presentations. A badly done mime or play is an embarrassment to the audience.

Bad performances in music or drama only continue, I might say, because of the good manners of those who watch them. If we had the brass neck to go up to the teacher in charge afterwards and say: "Well, old son, that was utterly excruciating, and I don't know how you had the cheek to put it on," then perhaps it would not happen so often. As it is, the principle holds good, as it does in so many fields of life, that the thick-skinned and incompetent survive and thrive on the forebearance and good nature of their fellows.

Incidentally, when it comes to putting on poor quality stuff, teachers come nowhere compared to those people who I might call "fringe educationists" — youth club leaders, Sunday School superintendents and the like.

Nativity Plays

The nativity play is often seen as the exclusive province of the youngest children, and certainly every infants school seems to put one on. If they are in luck there will be a photograph in the local paper, with a biblical caption. This is all the more likely if, as appears to be *de rigueur* at the moment, one of the three kings is really black, allowing us all to congratulate ourselves on what a civilized sort of country we live in.

The best sort of infant nativity play is the simplest, and the simplest is one where the children present a series of mimed scenes, perhaps with musical background, while a narrator reads out the Bible story. I long ago decided that as most nativity plays which have made-up dialogue suitable for children are unutterable banal, I would always prefer to stick to a formula of mime plus the words of the Bible.

I believe that very young children give a more convincing performance if they are freed from the added discipline of having to learn and present dialogue, and this means that they must mime. (No, they cannot make it up as they go along, and I hope to be preserved from those teachers who think they ought *and* from their productions.)

A child who only has to learn movements will learn them much more easily and much more convincingly than if he has to learn words as well, and the performance will be considerably more theatrical, and this, after all, is what we are talking about.

Mind you, the theatrical atmosphere in infant school plays is not helped by those mums who will insist on waving to their offspring. (It is a fallacy that the children wave first — they invariably know better.) In extreme cases I have known them actually to call encouragement, and on one never-to-be-forgotten occasion, to run forward with a cardigan to ward off the draught.

Secondary School Plays

It is in the secondary school, though, that the school play really comes into its own, because to the secondary school child there is nothing at all in the modern repertoire which is out of reach.

This, I hasten to say, does not mean that children should be given the opportunity to play every part of which they are capable. I admit to a feeling of hesitation about allowing an adolescent to reach out to a part which requires a great deal of sexual sophistication.

I do not think, for example, that many teachers would be happy about coaching a teenage girl in the part of Blanche in "Streetcar Named Desire".

(Yes, I know. I will receive letters from junior schools the length and breadth of the land saying that they have done the whole of Tennessee Williams and are hoping to start on the really hard stuff shortly.)

Problems of Putting on a Play

What about the business of actually putting on a school play? The teacher who volunteers to take on the responsibility is likely to have either a very thick skin, or be a masochist. Or he might be extremely naïve, taking the job on with shining hopes while his colleagues fall about and rub their hands with glee. Certainly from the moment he agrees to be in charge, he is committed to what is really nothing more than a particularly long-drawn-out nervous breakdown.

The wise teacher who is placed in this position will surround himself with a number of willing colleagues under the title of "Drama Committee". At the very first meeting someone should be taking notes. This is so that the teacher who, for instance, volunteers to make and paint sixty-three Inca breastplates can be held to his promise, and not conveniently deny all knowledge of it three days before the dress rehearsal.

By handling the drama committee correctly, at least some of the headaches can be shared, and others can sometimes be off-loaded altogether.

The working departments of the school should be brought in to display their special skills as much as possible. The needlework department, after going through the motions of protesting, can usually be relied upon to produce costumes The art department will paint scenery after the woodworkers have built it.

There might be schools where this sort of support is not forth-coming. If so, it might be as well to ask why. Perhaps there have been ructions in the past, or perhaps they have never been asked properly. In any event, a gentle and flattering approach might do wonders.

If recalcitrance is still evident, it is worth considering whether to abandon the idea of a play. There is not much point in a teacher flogging himself to death in the face of obstructionism from his own colleagues.

Obviously, this whole business is an exercise in personnel rela-tions of an order that would command a £14,000 a year salary in ICI or British Leyland. There will be temperamental flouncings, raving quarrels, outright resignations and rushings-off to the head who will, if he is wise, have locked himself in his private loo, emerging only to make a speech on the last night.

A cool head, a soft answer and a mention in the programme will solve most of the problems.

The teacher in charge will need a good business manager, and this should fall to the most efficient and well organized member of staff. Disasters on stage will normally pass unnoticed, unless the scenery actually plunges into the front row of the audience.

Front of house mistakes on the other hand, such as booking out the same block of seats to two sets of old-age pensioners, or failing to order enough bottles of milk for the refreshment teas, are almost impossible to cover up, and involve the actual comfort and well-being of the audience.

If in fact, I were a head and found that Lord Olivier had fallen on bad times and decided to come and teach in my school, I would welcome him with open arms and enrol him for the school play — to be in charge of the front of house arrangements. A man with his theatrical experience could not go wrong.

The play will also be more successful if the producer, director, teacher in charge — call him what you will — is either a first-rate scrounger, or has such a person at his beck and call. I have a colleague who fulfils this function absolutely infallibly. He has been known to produce, at the shortest notice, items as varied as two or three stuffed stags' heads, a dozen cork lifebelts, hundreds of yards of rope and unlimited supplies of beer glasses.

In this sort of thing, he was rivalled only by the P.E. master we had, who decided one afternoon that he would decorate the hall with parachutes for some reason that I forget. Within a couple of hours he came staggering up the drive bearing a great festoon of canvas webbing and nylon, having relieved the local parachute regiment of several apparently perfectly good parachutes. I still have minor nightmares at the thought of bold soldiery launching themselves into space on the end of yards of silk which had been draped over rafters and metal light fittings, and covered with little stars secured with safety pins.

For fairly obvious educational reasons, many producers like to involve as many children as possible in their school plays. A recent one which a colleague of mine put on was like this. It was a play with a lot of insect characters, and among other delights there was an ant army. This was made up of about fifty second-year boys and girls. At various points in the play they had to walk across the stage, round the side of the hall, in through the entrance doors, up the main gangway of the auditorium and up a ramp on to the stage again. The beauty of it was there were enough of them, with careful spacing, for this to be a continuous non-stop line, and as they made several circuits, on each appearance stamping their feet lustily and uttering various chants appropriate to an ant brigade, the effect was rather striking.

The disadvantage of having a large cast is, of course, that it is very difficult to keep under control, both in terms of gathering them together for rehearsals and in the sheer business of getting them to stand still and listen.

In the case of the ant army, my colleague had a nightmare task also in keeping them quiet during the actual performance. The exigencies of the hall were such that the children who were playing ant soldiers had to be secreted behind a sort of canvas dodger which was placed alongside the audience. This worked well at rehearsal, but on the first night the children were so feverishly excited that no amount of cajolery and threats would induce them to be silent. As a result, for several minutes at a time, the action on stage was totally inaudible because of the chattering, threats and dull thuds which came from behind the screen. They made so much noise in fact that they missed most of their cues, and the play was more than once held up for lack of ants, who were all too obviously pre-occupied a matter of inches away from the audience.

This particular play also ran into trouble over the set, and there is a lesson to be learned here also. The stage had been given a sort of all-enveloping drapery of muslin and paper to simulate an insect-type environment. This looked very effective, but the fire officer whose duty it is to inspect the arrangements at all public perform-ances, was displeased to the point of apoplexy. As a result, the stage staff spent a whole day painting every single bit of the drapes and decorations with flameproof solution.

Backstage Help

You can, of course, have lots of boys and girls involved in a play without them necessarily being all on the stage. Some of them can help with the stage management and lighting, but the wise teacher will make sure that there is a responsible member of staff in very close charge of such operations. The kind of boys who tend to gravitate towards scene shifting and electrical work are usually the ones who are prone to become involved in disastrous happenings of an explosive or mirth-provoking nature.

I knew a school production where the member of staff in charge

backstage spent the whole production trying to prevent his stage
hands from igniting the show with their discarded fag ends. As
soon as the lights went down, all the lads lit up, so that the backstage area looked like a national convention of demented glow-
worms, and they could smell tobacco smoke three rows back in
the audience which, as the play was set in a convent, did nothing
to add to the realism.

This business of scene shifting, incidentally, needs careful planning if the audience are not to be kept waiting for long periods of
time. The same colleague of mine who became involved with the
insects put on, at a previous school, a production of "Charley's
Aunt". The trouble was that there were only the most limited
facilities and a makeshift stage, and every change of scene had to
be effected by moving all the stage props in and out through one
door of standard classroom size. As "Charley's Aunt" includes,
among other things, a piano, this resulted in the most excruciating-
ly long pauses between scenes, punctuated by long drawn-out
scrapings, bangings, groans and curses. Another difficulty was that
the actors, once they had entered the backstage area and the
audience were in their places, were trapped as there was no separate stagedoor entrance. Boys who became desperate to go to the
toilet had to be lowered several floors on a rope from a small
window.

The Time and Place

Most schools find that the timing of a school play, in the sense of
deciding which part of the school year is most suitable, requires a
great deal of thought, and there are a number of limiting factors.
The timing of public examinations may well be a very powerful
decisive influence, and if the hall does not adequately black out
in daylight, then this too will have to be taken into account. It
behoves therefore, the enthusiastic putter-on of school plays to
consult his colleagues and the headmaster very carefully, and when
a date has been decided, to have this publicized as widely and as
soon as possible so that rival attractions will not be planned for the
same time.

Many schools, especially those which were built during periods of financial lavishness — and there were such times — are excellently equipped for the mounting of dramatic productions, with a large, curtained stage, a lighting board and all the backstage apparatus necessary for a very professional production. It is sad when one comes across such a set-up lying idle for want of an experienced or enthusiastic teacher to put it to good use, especially when there are other schools, perhaps in the same district, where a keen dramatist is having to make do with rostrum blocks and such lighting equipment as he can codge up in the workshops and laboratories. A little more interchange and co-operation between schools seems to be called for in a situation like this, but the lack of communication between separate establishments is one of the faults of our educational system.

There are drama teachers, of course, who dislike the limitations of the formal theatrical layout and prefer to work in a flexible setting, using the outdoor spaces and rearranging the hall perhaps so that, in the ultimate case, the audience sits on the stage and the play is performed on the floor. This is all to the good, of course, because putting on a school play is an exercise in educational theatre, and it is quite legitimate to make it experimental or difficult simply for the sake of the thing. In this way the minds of the actors and their audience can be stretched beyond the conventional limits, which is what education is all about.

For this sort of reason, schools of the future, while being lavishly equipped with theatrical equipment, should have it arranged in such a way that there is the possibility of great flexibility in the way it is used.

5
Outdoor Activities

Not so long ago, outdoor activities were seen as the great panacea for all adolescent ills. It was recognized that formal P.E. and organized games were failing to appeal to many youngsters and so, in the colleges of education, students were being instructed in the arts of mountaineering, camping and canoeing, so that they could lead children on to better things by way of a few freezing nights under canvas and a couple of duckings in the Grand Union Canal. The whole thing was somewhat reminiscent of the hiking craze which "swept" (as they say) through Britain in pre-war years and the Nazis' "Strength through Joy" movement.

The thinking behind it all was that the older pupil in school, and the young person at work, would find through outdoor activities some of the adventure which he craved and yet was denied by modern living. His predecessors had drawn bows at Agincourt, or shot down Heinkels over Kentish hop fields. He was deprived of this and therefore it should be replaced by canoe trips down the Wye or light camping in the Black Mountains.

It was hoped — indeed assumed — that young adolescents would thus be caused to go off and get their hair cut, dress in blazers and flannels, and eschew the smashing-up of bus shelters and the mugging of elderly citizens.

It was with this sort of philosophy in mind that the Outward Bound schools came into being, and later the Duke of Edinburgh's Award Scheme.

Within these idealistic terms of reference a degree of failure was inevitable. In general, only the converted were converted. The boys and girls who received their award from the Duke, or who proudly sported their Outward Bound ties were, and are, in too many cases, from middle-class homes and backgrounds. The mass salvation of the lost souls of the cafés and street corners has not occurred. It was a brave attempt though, and we must all stand in awe and respect of the enormous amount of effort that has been made by all those concerned, whether professionals or hard-working amateurs.

In fact, if we can forget the missionary crusading aspects of what we might call the Outdoor Movement, then there has in fact been a great deal of success in terms of giving pleasure and adventure to thousands of youngsters under expert and enthusiastic guidance.

Today, the missionary spirit is less evident. Everyone has the thing in perspective, and it is possible to evaluate outdoor activities in terms of what they have to offer to school children without becoming bogged down in their sociological implications as substitutes for the urban jungle battleground.

There are not many secondary schools which do not have some sort of outdoor activity going on. We can include under this heading: canoeing, camping, climbing, sailing, and all those pastimes which take children away from the streets and out into closer contact with the open air. In some cases this is all done through a well organized outdoor club catering for a wide range of such activities. In others there is just an enthusiastic teacher who takes groups of children to share in the one particular activity which most interests him.

An enthusiastic teacher is indeed the prime requisite, more important than any amount of sophisticated equipment. This sort of out-of-school activity is probably more time-consuming than any other. Long evenings will have to be spent on preparation work, or on the construction of boats or canoes, and there will be many weekends which are given over wholly or in part to leading expeditions.

In addition to enthusiasm, though, knowledge is also essential. In this field, lack of specialized knowledge can result in children, at worst, being exposed to mortal danger and at best being made to suffer unnecessary discomfort. Ignorant enthusiasm might suffice in some of the out-of-school activities under discussion, but in the field of outdoor activities it will not do. Fortunately, though, the ignorant can be taught, and there are enough courses and holiday schools which set out to do this very thing, and to ensure that at least the basic rules of comfort and safety are adhered to.

At this point I intend to look at one or two of the traditional outdoor pursuits in a little more detail.

Camping

This is, of course, the basic activity, because so many of the others assume a knowledge of camping, or are themselves made more pleasurable if the facilities exist for camping. I have no intention of telling people how to go camping — or how to do any of the other activities, for that matter. There are plenty of books on the subject. What I will do is to see how one particular teacher managed to start off camping as an activity in his school.

It is significant that this teacher is not by any means a physical educationist. It is not all that common these days to find a P.E. specialist who has a particular interest in outdoor activities, such has been the swing of the pendulum. This one is in fact a graduate chemistry specialist. It would be easy to suggest that the spending of long periods cooped up in close proximity to hydro-whatsit acid and iron filings is enough to drive anyone to the hills. In any event and whatever the reason, there are not many weekends during the whole year when Robinson is not off to the moors and valleys with a party of youngsters.

When he arrived at the school, nothing was going on in the way of outdoor activities. It was rumoured that some years before, in the régime of a previous head, a large amount of equipment, to the value of several hundred pounds, had been purchased. If this was so, by the time Robinson arrived the stuff had totally disappeared, down to the last tent peg. This sort of thing happens depressingly often, and is one reason why some school heads and authorities are reluctant to buy large quantities of capital equipment for out-of-school activities.

It might happen, for instance, that a teacher buys canoes and then leaves, to be followed by someone who cannot tell a canoe from an aircraft carrier, but who spends a lot of money on tents. He may then be succeeded in turn by a teacher who is anxious to restart canoeing but who finds that the canoes have deteriorated from neglect to the point where they can no longer be used.

This sort of situation really ought not to arise. Even if equipment is temporarily out of use, its safe-keeping and maintenance ought to be possible, merely by dint of the head giving somebody the job of doing it.

In any event, because of all this, Robinson decided that it would be best to prove that camping was actually going on before pleading for funds to buy tents and equipment. He had some bits and pieces of his own, and there were numerous willing friends. Most important, though, was the discovery that the local education authority operated, through the P.E. organizer's office, a loan scheme whereby it was possible for schools to hire out camping equipment. The first time the teacher hired some of this, he was subjected to very close scrutiny. Clearly the authority was not going to be a party to sending off children into the wide blue yonder unless they were led and looked after by someone who knew what he was doing. They wanted to know everything, so Robinson said, except the state of his love life.

The camping activities could have gone on indefinitely using this equipment, but there were certain disadvantages, and although the hire service was ideal for a newly formed group or a school which had no hope of raising the cash for their own staff, it would nevertheless be better to try to buy some equipment. The main consideration was that the hire equipment was heavily used and therefore needed to be booked a long time in advance. The booking also had to specify every single item, and this necessitated a degree of long range planning which was not always practical; the number of pupils likely to be attending a camp, for instance, could fluctuate right up to the day of departure. In addition, it was felt that having control of their own equipment would enable the boys and girls to learn more about its correct maintenance and the reasons for the choice of particular items. There was also the natural desire for independence.

Still, for a year, the camping club operated on hired equipment, supplemented by borrowed items. The first expedition was a walking outing in Wales. This was a day trip only, and one of the objectives was to find a camping site which could be used for a later weekend trip. This developed as the normal pattern — first a one-day reconnaissance and later a camp — so that as time went by a "store" of camp sites was built up, each one with the advantage of having had personal inspection and personal contact with the owner. Within a remarkably short time, reliable camping sites were available in most of the scenic regions of England and Wales.

Robinson opened his camping activities as a club, with membership open to boys and girls in the middle and upper schools of the comprehensive school in which he taught. The members paid 25p a year, and on top of this paid for each camp which they attended. The school was fortunate in having its own vehicle — a van, converted into a fourteen seater minibus — and this meant that transport costs were kept down. In fact for a weekend's camping, from Friday evening to Sunday, the cost per child never exceeded £1.50. The teacher in charge always bought catering packs of food from a wholesale cash and carry, finding that with careful portion control this was very economical. On some weekends he even managed to make a small profit.

The local education authority in which he worked, like all others, had a set of rules about trips out of school. These were written out clearly in the handbook of regulations, and Robinson found that in order to keep within them, the main responsibilities which lay upon him were to see that there was adequate supervision — laid down in the regulations as a ratio of staff to pupils of about one to ten, with modifications in certain circumstances — and also to see that there was proper insurance cover. This was arranged through a local broker and the arrangements for the expeditions had to be explained to him well in advance. When the club had run for a year, it was decided that it was unnecessary to make payments for each outing, but that an annual policy would be provided, with a premium to be paid at the end of the year based on the number of camps undertaken.

When the existence of the club was firmly established — and it soon had eighty members, making it the largest single activity group in the school — money was forth-coming from the school fund and from the parents' association, for the purchase of tents and other equipment. Robinson kept the cost down by going to commercial tent hire firms at the end of the season and asking if they had any tents to sell. In this way he was able to buy good quality and little-used equipment at just about exactly half the original cost.

Through the camping club, a lot of children were given their first taste of life under canvas. Most of the members had never camped before, and were fairly aghast at the contrast between a Welsh hillside and a block of council flats. One boy was also staggered by his first sight of stew which had grass floating about in it, and vowed that he would never stray beyond the city boundary again. On the whole, though, they settled down very well.

Mixed camping became possible when one or two lady members of staff volunteered to accompany the expeditions. The girls were even less experienced in the great outdoors than the boys. The major problem with girls new to camping is always a tendency to take along suitcases containing large amounts of unsuitable clothing, including flimsy negligées and high-heeled shoes, no matter how much warning they are given beforehand. A camp which has personable young ladies in it, or in some parts of the country any sort of young ladies, is likely to be beset by prowling youths from nearby villages. Scenes develop like those in exploration films, where the tents are surrounded by fires to keep off the wolves, and the intrepid heroes take turns to stay up all night with rifles in their laps.

Canoeing

The development of canoeing in this country as a popular outdoor pursuit owes an enormous amount to the work of Percy Blandford, whose books on canoeing, and ideas on canoe design, ought to be well looked at by anyone new to the subject, even if he then goes on to develop his own ideas or to adopt those of others.

The traditional way of starting canoeing in a school is firstly to interest some boys and girls in the subject, perhaps by showing them a film or taking them to look at, and perhaps have trips in, some canoes belonging to co-operative friends or colleagues. Then they are asked to buy proprietary canoe kits (not complete canoes — it takes a lot of the satisfaction out of the business) and are supervised during their work on them, which is best done, if the co-operation is there, in the school woodwork department.

All you need then is some water. Rivers are liable to be difficult because of the varying amount of control which exists over their use. The Wye is easier than most, which is why you cannot sit on its banks for long without seeing at least one school canoeing party come thrashing past in the final throes of exhaustion. For perhaps the majority of schools, the nearest usable water will be a canal, and provided that licences are obtained from the local waterways office, using them is comparatively free of formalities and problems.

The great value of the canoe is its portability and it is this which makes it possible to sample every sort of canoeing water from smelly urban canals to sparkling Scottish rivers, and perhaps the sea itself if the canoes are suitable and the leader experienced.

To take advantage of this mobility, it will be necessary sooner or later to devise some means of transport. Canoes are light in weight but rather unwieldy. (Which reminds me of a college friend who built a canoe during his course and then took it home

on the train to East Anglia, with several changes en route. It only
needed the cameras to have been there and yet another classic
comedy silent would have been at the National Film Theatre.) The
best canoe transporter is a specially built trailer carrying six or
eight canoes in two banks three or four high. A resourceful and
well-intentioned metalwork teacher should be capable of building
one of these on a cheaply bought trailer chassis. This is yet another
demonstration of how neccessary it is that the successful organizer
of out-of-school activities should be adept and resourceful in the
handling of human relationships.

A large canoe expedition could be transported by furniture van.
A few telephone chats with local firms might result in a surprisingly cheap rate being negotiated — canoes are child's play compared with wardrobes and grand pianos. The possibility should not
be neglected, either, of there being a child in school who hails
from a furniture removing family.

Sailing

The problem to overcome with this activity lies in the fact that a
sailing boat, while being expensive, will only accommodate two or
three children at a time. The sheer attraction of sailing, though, is
such that it is very popular in schools, and is growing in strength
all the time.

Some schools have their own boats. Banbury School, for instance, which is just one that I happen to know about, is able to
mount an inter-house regatta. Not many schools have their own
inland water or slipway facilities, but Banbury solves this problem,
as do others, through the friendship and hospitality of the local
sailing club.

If there is no local Schools Sailing Association, then the obvious
thing for any teacher who wants to introduce the sport, is to
approach local sailing clubs. It may be possible for the school boat
to be incorporated into the club, or at least to be accommodated
there; it will therefore need to be one of the types of boats which
make up the club fleet, if it is to take part in club races. The purchase of the boat may be facilitated through the club, and indeed

a secondhand boat at a reasonable price may be forthcoming, because sailing clubs are usually keen to see their sport introduced to young people. The boys and girls who become interested may find themselves taken on as crews for racing by club members. The member who sails to the start with a thirteen-year-old girl as his crew on a calm day will feel he has an advantage over the boats which carry two fourteen stone over-fed executives.

It is worth the while of an interested teacher to enquire whether or not there is any School Sailing Association in his area. Birmingham, for instance, which must surely be worse off for available sailing water than practically any other large authority in the country, has one, and a fair number of schools are members. The importance of such an association is not lessened when there are fewer available facilities. It becomes a major function of the organization to see that what there is, is known about and used, and to explore the possibility of improving the position.

One of the things which such an association will try to do is to help its member schools in the correct training of staff and pupils in the basics of sailing, and to supervise the sharing of sailing time when space and facilities are limited. In some areas they also organize the sharing of boats, so that if seven schools have a boat each, then each school can have the use of seven boats for a half day each week. This is yet another example of the advantages which are to be gained from co-operation between schools.

Other Activities

There are other sorts of outdoor activity, of course. I know, for instance, that the boys of King Henry VIII School in Coventry go off orienteering, not only in this country but also on the continent. This sport is well worth investigating in that, at least in its early stages, it can succeed in putting some interest into cross-country running — and it is not always the fastest runners who win.

Rock climbing I will say very little about, because it will never be attempted by any teacher who has not had considerably more experience, of the hardest practical kind, than I have had.

In the vast majority of cases, the schoolboy rock climber will gain his experience either in a club outside school, or on a specialist course.

6
Trips and Outings

The School Trip has always been with us. At one time, so we are told by those who were around then, it consisted of a wagonette ride to the nearest field, followed by a picnic and many earnest discussions among the knickerbockered children as to whether dandelions really did make you wet the bed.

The point was, though, that a School Trip really meant what it said, All the school went at once; teachers, children, caretaker, lots of parents and the inevitable vicar or two. This custom prevailed well into the era of the charabanc and the excursion train, and you would be treated to the spectacle of hundreds of little Birmingham urchins strung out along the Malvern Hills like characters in a very deep Polish film.

Outings like this are probably a little less common now, although I know a junior school which only recently went en masse on a canal trip. The teachers spent the whole day narrowly preventing a tragic mass drowning, and have since declared that they will only repeat the performance if the boat is totally enclosed with half inch mesh wire netting.

The usual pattern today, is for a number of different trips and outings to take place from any one school in a year, with each occasion perhaps being less of an earth-shattering even for the youngsters than such things used to be.

This new approach to "The School Trip" is partly because children are usually better travelled than were earlier generations, and it is not so necessary to take them just anywhere for the sake of it. In addition, with the trend towards a more outward-looking curriculum in most schools, journeys out of school for specific educational purposes have become more common. There

is not the idea so much of a year's hard slogging, heads down in
the classroom, followed by a day at the sea or in the country.

A school outing today is more often planned with at least some
consideration for the work the children have been doing, even if it
is not really an integrated part of their studies, and failing even
this, there will be some thought for the educational value of what
the children are going to see.

A Birmingham junior school works a system where each class
spends a year on an inter-disciplinary project. One year, for
instance, each of the four years of the school studied under the
titles of the four ancient elements — earth, air, fire and water. It
seemed a logical step for the class which had been studying water
to visit the hills of mid-Wales, where the theft of Welsh water by
the arrogant imperialistic English actually takes place; and for the
air groups to go to Heathrow Airport. The opportunities are
obvious enough.

Organization

Trips out of school are probably more frequent at secondary than
at junior level. The reason is simply that it is easier, in practical
terms, to take children out of secondary school than it is to take
them out of a junior school. In a junior school there will be, by
and large, one teacher per class, with each class probably having
upwards of thirty children in it. A teacher who wants to take a
class out of school will, therefore, by doing so, denude another
class of its teacher. This is inevitable, because it would be fool-
hardy, to say nothing of being against the rules of most local
authorities, for a teacher to attempt any sort of outing further
than the front door in sole charge of more than about twenty
children.

Any class trip in a junior school therefore causes repercussions
throughout the rest of the school which may involve, if a class
cannot be covered by the head or any visiting or part-time staff
who may happen to be around, the splitting up of a group of
children and their dispersion among other classes. This is obviously
not satisfactory, and it is possible to achieve a state of affairs where
one class is out on the Long Mynd or in the Whispering Gallery

having its education enhanced; while, as a direct result, another class back at school is being retarded by missing a day of its normal routine.

In a large secondary school, on the other hand, with the more generous staffing ratios that our masters deem to be appropriate, there will be, at any one time, a number of teachers having a free period. By calling on them through the day, the missing teacher can be covered with the minimum of inconvenience. As a result, it is quite literally true that a class in a large comprehensive school can go on an outing without being missed by the rest of the school.

If you add to this the fact that such a school may well prepare children for external examinations which call for a specific amount of field work in certain subjects, then it is not so surprising that a child stands more chance of doing some zooming off over the horizon when he is in secondary school than he did when in junior school.

As a working example of the approach of one school to the organization of school outings, I have looked at what happens in one large comprehensive school.

This is a school of about twelve hundred pupils organized into lower, middle and upper schools. A few years ago the head of middle school (which comprises the third and fourth years) felt that the practice whereby each teacher organized an outing for his own form in a fairly haphazard way during the summer term could be improved upon to the benefit not only of the children, but of the staff and the general running of the school.

He called a meeting of middle school form teachers at which he suggested that all "pleasure" trips in the middle school, as distinct from those organized to illustrate a particular point on the curriculum of a subject, should take place on the same day. The aim was to concentrate the total amount of pandemonium into one frenetic twelve hours, after which the teachers would be more or less free to lurch around the place glassy-eyed for the remaining dying days of the summer term.

The idea met with general approval. One day is as good as another, it was felt, for most trips, and it was always accepted that if there were pressing reasons for holding a particular outing on a different day the system would remain flexible enough to allow this.

From that point it was only a short step to the complete integration of the whole thing, so that instead of each class going off on its own trip, details of all available outings could be announced to the children who would then choose which one they wanted to go on.

This gave them much more freedom of choice than they had previously experienced, and there was also a degree of freedom of choice for the teachers. The head of the middle school proposed to make a mass coach booking and to collect all the money himself, which relieved the teachers of an irksome chore.

There are some teachers who do not mind handling money — I am not one of them. I have a sinking feeling whenever I sit down to count money I have collected for a school function. It glares up at me malevolently from the table, and I know without any question of doubt that there will be at least a fiver short. Time and time again I have found that if I have to count a pile of money which should come to £40, I will reach £32 with an uneasy awareness that there are only a couple of tenpenny pieces and a scattering of bronze left. Ugh!

I well understood then the gratitude of the staff of the comprehensive school when the head of middle school relieved his colleagues of this particular burden.

When the basics of the outing plan were decided, the middle school form teachers had a hilarious ten minutes trying to find a name for the project. Some of those suggested were, while being graphically accurate, a little too lacking in delicacy for outside consumption, being centred around the habit which some children have on coach outings, of failing to keep secure the contents of their stomachs. Eventually, though, the eminently sensible "Middle School on the Move" came into being.

The next problem, and a recurring one which had to be faced every year, was to decide on seven or eight destinations for the various trips. The pattern then and in later years was to offer an assortment of attractions; some involving energetic walking over hills; some fairly directly educational, with visits to canals and museums and things; and one to London, to cater for the minority of children who still had not seen the standard sights.

Supervision

The teachers then had to sort themselves out so that there were
at least two of them on each trip, including at least one lady
teacher. This is a sensible sort of arrangement, and is usually given
the force of a ruling by the education authority, who insist that

there shall be a ratio of about one staff to twenty children, and
that there be a lady on any trip where girls are involved.

There can be problems if the ratio of men to women on the
staff is unbalanced, as in fact it is at the school which we are
looking at. Since the lowering of the age of majority, one way
round this might be to take along an eighteen-year-old sixth
former, who is an adult, and therefore ought to be qualified to
take this responsibility. The legal rights and wrongs of doing this
are not firmly established, but it is worth taking up the point
with the local education authority. A number of schools are
certainly exploring the position at the moment.

At one of them, in fact, the biology master had organized a
long weekend's field study for a mixed party. He was to be
accompanied by a lady colleague who happened to be ill on the
day of departure. No other lady was immediately available, and
the senior mistress resorted to going round the school approaching
senior girls and saying; "Er, Sandra, what are you doing between

now and next Tuesday?" One of them went in the end, and the legal position was rendered foolproof by gazetting her as having left, an event which was imminent.

This sorting out of staff for "Middle School on the Move" tends, I am told, to give rise to the sort of hilarity where a schoolmaster bursts into the head's room saying, "Quick, I need a woman urgently!"

Once each party has its leaders, it becomes the job of them both to decide on a programme of activities for the day out. Inclinations vary, but the opinion has grown that it is a mistake to try to pack in too much. A day spent in rushing from one museum to another, or from a stately home to a zoo with fifteen minutes for lunch is nerve-racking for both children and staff.

A typical "Middle School on the Move" outing a couple of years ago was to Liverpool. It seems that no one could quite remember whose idea it was to go there, but the leaders assigned to it wrote off and fixed up a visit to the Roman Catholic Cathedral, resisting the temptation to go to the docks as well, on the principle that one leisurely visit is better than two rushed ones.

As it happened there was time in the afternoon to take the children to New Brighton and let them loose for an hour. This caused some amusement, because New Brighton is essentially a weekend resort and it was deserted on the day they visited. The children more or less had to shake the amusement park attendants awake, and as far as the eye could see down the prom and the main street there were groups of middle school pupils desultorily wandering about looking for the action.

This particular trip was rather too long, involving a four-hour coach journey. Anything over about two and a half hours is a little too much for everyone's nerves and staying powers, and if the children start to be a bit awkward, the journey seems endless.

Behaviour

The business of behaviour on school outings is quite critical. It is very necessary to achieve a friendly atmosphere between staff and pupils — they are going to have to spend the whole day together and co-operation is essential. If a situation develops where the teachers have to crack the whip, a surly atmosphere can result, and this means, inevitably, a spoilt day. Nothing short of experience can help a teacher to avoid this situation.

The usual mistake is to forget that the children will be more exuberant than usual and that some allowance will have to be made for this. This means that it is necessary to discover the thin line between tolerance of what is really nothing more than high spirits, and weakness in the face of cheek.

A young teacher who takes a party out would do well because of this to see to it that the other teacher is an experienced and well-respected member of staff who can provide a good degree of support.

Most schools of my experience are satisfied with the way their children behave when they go out of school. This is not so surprising. Children do appreciate that an effort is being made to give them an enjoyable day, and if there is a little give and take in the face of their initial excitement, then everything normally settles down well.

It is a little puzzling, then, to hear so many stories from tourist spots of badly behaved school parties. They may well exist, of course; a very tiny percentage of poorly organized children dashing about a public place can create an impression far out of proportion to their numbers. On the whole, though, I suspect unsympathetic adults of mistaking childish glee and high spirits for anti-social behaviour.

As an example of this, I once took a party to a certain show-place in the London area. The children, all second formers in a secondary modern school, poured across the drive in front of the place and hurried up the steps, where they waited chattering noisily and excitedly while I contacted the guide inside. He took one look at them and said "Obstreperous lot aren't they?"

I ought to have walked away or knocked him down or something, but being of a pacific nature, I contented myself with a mild protest. Children are subjected to so much of this sort of thing by the public at large that it says a great deal for their resilience that they ever grow up normally.

Guides in public buildings have so much contact with school parties that you would think they would know how to talk to children by now, but they vary enormously in their ability to keep youngsters interested.

In the worst cases, the party comes up against a sleepy individual who drones on in a monotone audible only to those standing within a radius of two feet. In a situation like this the teacher often finds himself having to prowl round the edges of the group, nudging and frowning at the ones who are most openly inattentive. Some colleagues are more tolerant of their charges, and believe that if a guide cannot hold the interest of the children he deserves all he gets, but I am not personally convinced of the essential humanity of this approach.

There are, though, many people outside teaching who cannot seem to grasp that the modern child is not one to stand in abject silence simply because he is being spoken to by an adult. He will only do it if the adult has something to say.

The guides at St Paul's Cathedral all wear things that look like cassocks, and the last time I took a party there the children assumed that the young man who showed them round was of the cloth. Afterwards they kept coming up to me and saying things like: "Please, sir, that vicar called me a little bastard" or, "Please, sir, that vicar asked me for a fag."

Freedom

I mentioned that the teacher in charge of the Liverpool trip had given the children an hour of freedom in New Brighton. It is always difficult to know exactly how much freedom to give. It comes down in the end, I suppose, to commonsense and experience. Some teachers will not let their parties disperse at all, and considering the amount of responsibility involved, it is difficult to blame them.

A lot depends, of course, on the age of the children. In the case of a stop at a motorway service station, for instance, a junior school party leader would probably want to escort the children across the car park and try to keep them in view most of the time. With fourteen year olds, on the other hand, it might be more usual to say: "Back in fifteen minutes. Mind the traffic on the car park, and watch the prices."

On a trip to London I once allowed a party of thirteen and fourteen year olds to go off unsupervised for about two hours. I had written permission from their parents to do this, and I gave them a sketch map each and a duplicated list of hints, warnings and information about things to look at. With these children, and being in London, I think I was at the borderline of the amount of freedom which is allowable. Indeed, some colleagues disagreed with me, although a teacher of my acquaintance once let a party loose in the Casbah in Tangiers.

I am not sure I did the right thing on that London trip, though. Not because of the risk of any mishap, but because I feel that the children would have gained more from their two hours if they had been taken round and shown things. Most of them in fact just mooched around as they do at home.

Methods of Travel

So far, as regards the actual travelling arrangements for outings, I have assumed that the main form of transport is by coach. I see no reason to doubt that this is the most convenient method. The coach picks you up where and when you want, and the cost is competitive with anything else. A friendly and co-operative driver is a great asset, and it is a good idea to remember the name of such a one when you come across him, and to ask for him when you book again with the same firm. I have noticed, incidentally, a growing habit for coaches to display a plaque inside saying something like: "Introducing your driver, SID." How nice it would be if we did that in our classrooms at the beginning of the year: "Introducing your teacher, Dennis 'Baggybritches' Malone."

Rail travel is sometimes convenient between major towns, and you can usually do a package deal with coach travel at each end. This is less wearing when the journey is very long, but the cost is almost always higher than doing the whole thing by coach.

And what about flying? Some travel agents will do a day trip to Paris or Rotterdam, with coach travel at each end and a courier to take you round the sights for about £12 a head. Dates are usually limited to the period outside the peak holiday season, but if you can arrange something convenient, and also make sure to gain the maximum educational benefit by working in conjunction with interested departments of the school, then such a trip can be very worthwhile.

I should mention that while the travel agent will include the cost of insurance cover when he quotes for this, or indeed any trip, it is worth checking that what he offers is in line with the requirements of the local education authority, for some are stricter than others in this respect.

Obviously a teacher who organizes any sort of outing should make himself familiar with the rules of the authority and inform them well beforehand that the trip is going to take place. This is particularly important if there is what the lawyers and insurance bods would call "more than the normal amount of risk". This includes things like air travel, climbing and skin diving.

It is also necessary to make absolutely certain that every child going on a trip out of school has the permission of his parents. Some schools have an arrangement whereby any child going on an outing takes home a printed consent slip to be signed and brought back before he can go.

Precautions

The leader of a party on an outing should have with him a list not just of the names of the children but also of their addresses and telephone numbers as well. As a demonstration of the need for this, I heard of a party of senior boys and girls who were on a trip to London. A theatre visit was included. One of the boys disappeared during the afternoon and did not turn up at the theatre. This was fairly worrying, but he might just have been more interested in finding his own amusement than in going to the theatre. The real worry started when he did not turn up at the coach at midnight for the return journey. After waiting some time, the leader of the party phoned the head of the school for advice. The head said: "Leave him, and I will go round to his house to tell the parents. Where does he live?" See what I mean?

Having to face the possibility of a member of the party being adrift is the nightmare of every school trip organizer, and it is difficult to give general advice about it because every case is likely to be different. By all means talk to the police, but they will not normally be as worried as you are, especially in the case of older children, because whereas an hour's absence will have reduced you to panic, it will not really be a long enough period to cause the police to take much action.

Telephoning the head for advice is clearly a good way of sharing the responsibility, and the party leader must make sure that he has the head's home telephone number.

It may ultimately be necessary for one member of staff to stay behind. In this case he should make sure that he has enough money to effect the succour and retrieval not only of himself but of the errant child.

Young children — say of junior school age — should never be allowed to stray far enough to make disappearance a likely possibility. Constant vigilance usually works, and most children are sufficiently worried themselves about getting lost to prevent them from doing so. Disappearances are fortunately *very* rare.

It is worth remembering that vanishing teenage girls in London are usually to be found in Carnaby Street looking disappointed with it all. Boys who skip off usually go to look at Wembley Stadium, thinking it to be two minutes walk from Trafalgar Square. Escapees have usually discussed their plans on the coach journey, and some close questioning may well provide the answer.

It is worth giving a little thought to the question of first-aid. The organizer could take a box of materials, although most coaches are fitted out with a first-aid kit. The general rule that it is best to err on the side of caution applies here as much as anywhere else. If a child appears to be seriously ill or injured then a trip to hospital is called for; this is another reason for wanting his home address and telephone number, as the hospital will want to contact the parents if their permission is needed for any treatment.

I heard only the other day of a boy who was bitten on the hand by a rat while on a visit to a farm. It is difficult to envisage anything much more unlikely and yet right out of the blue a young teacher was faced with the necessity of doing something about it.

Rat bites are potentially dangerous, and in this case the aid of the coach driver was enlisted to take the boy to the hospital.

Having made all the preparations, I feel the important thing about any school trip is that everyone should enjoy themselves, and no one can do this if the teacher presents a panic stricken aspect all the time. However he feels, he should look happy and relaxed!

Holidays Abroad

School holiday trips abroad are best organized through one of the travel agencies which specialize in this sort of thing. There are quite a lot of them and they nearly all send their brochures to schools each year. Study them all, and try to talk to a teacher who has used the services of the one which interests you — if necessary, obtain the address of such a teacher from the agent, who should be perfectly willing to help in this way.

The rest is largely commonsense. The only point which is likely to give trouble is knowing how much freedom to give to the children, and there are no quick answers to this, with so many variables involved. It is worth trying to give as much freedom as seems reasonable, because the children will be disappointed if they are herded around all the time as they are at school.

It is quite likely that they won't show a great deal of enthusiasm for the standard tourist sights, and this should be remembered. There is a good Times Educational Supplement cartoon which shows a school party outside Notre Dame. All the children have their backs to the gesticulating guide and are watching a chap digging up the road with a pneumatic drill. Every school party leader would do well to take into account the "pneumatic drill factor" when planning a holiday abroad.

7
Educational Cruising

A long time has passed since I was on a troopship. It was called *Empire Orwell,* and I went out to Malaya on it during the post-war emergency. Troopships had an atmosphere (and I use that word advisedly) all their own. The *Orwell's* particular speciality was, as I recall, a crew which was almost completely made up of queer Irishmen. During the voyage I was forced, for the first and last time in my life, to defend my honour, a feat of arms which I accomplished in the night bakery with the aid of a potato peeler.

What has all this to do with education? Apart from the fact that it could be said that I received as much education in three weeks on the *Orwell* as I had in eight years at school, the main connection lies in the fact that some of the troopships whose names were so familiar to us (not the *Empire Orwell* itself, as far as I know though) have entered in more recent times upon a new lease of life as educational cruise ships.

The leading operator in this field is the British India Steam Navigation Company, a member of the P & O Group. This company operates two ships, SS *Nevasa* and SS *Uganda*, cruising mainly in the Mediterranean region, with calls at Iberian and North African Ports.

The educational aims and advantages are obvious. Not only do the children have the chance to see things which are normally only pictures in a book or shadows on a projection screen, but they do so in the company of their own friends and teachers and in a way which is professionally organized down to the last detail.

In order to see how such a cruise is run, and to understand the advantages and the snags, I propose to examine an actual cruise, organized and led by a geography teacher whom I will call Mr Smith.

A Typical Cruise

Smith decided in the spring of 1972 to lead a party of pupils
from the comprehensive school in which he teaches on a cruise at
Christmas. He found out about cruising when a letter addressed
to the school from British India Steam Navigation was directed
to him.

"I had," he said, "just come back from taking a party camping
over the Easter holidays, and for weeks afterwards any piece of
paper about travel of any sort found its way into my pigeon hole."

Normally, the plans for a cruise would be laid a little earlier
than they were in this case. What had happened was that the
company had put on an extra cruise after revising its schedules,
and then written to schools to tell them about it. Smith reckons
you should really start thinking about it at least a year before
actually travelling. There is a fair amount of competition for
bookings, and more and more education authorities are taking
up block bookings for well into the future. These block bookings
are then farmed out to the schools within their area. In this way,
smaller schools, or those with only a comparatively few interested
pupils, can take part by combining with others.

After reading the letter, Smith replied, expressing interest, and
received in return a detailed set of literature. The cruise in
question was to be to Madeira, Teneriffe, Las Palmas and Lisbon,
and was to cost about £60 per child. He added to this sum enough
to cover the cost of insurance and of travel to and from Southampton, where the cruise was to start, and a little for emergencies, and
quoted a cost to the pupils of £68 a head.

A large number of boys and girls expressed interest, but Smith
was not altogether optimistic that there would be a large response
when it came to bringing along the £5 initial deposit which he
requested, because the economic climate in the area was no
better than that of anywhere else at the time: redundancy and
short-time working were either realities or nasty prospects for
many parents, and there was reluctance to commit money for the
future.

Nevertheless, thirty-nine deposits came in within a day or two
of the announcement, and it says a great deal for the foresight

both of parents who did book and of those who might have liked to but did not, that during the months which followed there were only seven withdrawals, all because of unforeseen difficulties.

The company gives free passage to teachers as party leaders in the ratio of one adult to fifteen children in secondary schools.

Thus on this cruise, there were to be two free places. In the event, though, four members of staff decided to go, and as it was clear that all of them would have some share in the supervision of the children, some private arrangement was made between them about the distribution of the costs. It is worth noting that by doing this, a number of colleagues can have a pleasant though hard-working holiday at a very reasonable cost.

As soon as bookings were made and deposits sent in, the Company sent a representative to the school who showed a film and talked to the parents of the prospective travellers.

After that began the long hard slog of collecting the money. Predictably, it was much more difficult for some parents than it was for others. The employment position became worse rather than better as the weeks went by, and inflation eroded away at family purses. Nevertheless, the money did come in steadily, and was recorded on payment cards kept by the children.

Insurance proved a little bit of a problem in this particular case. The company provides a standard form of insurance through specialist insurers, but it was found that their policy did not meet in every detail the requirements of the particular local education authority in which the school is situated, which is particularly stringent about regulations and insurance for out-of-school activities.

This should be a signal to anyone who organizes an out-of-school activity which involves insurance. Just because an outside organization, such as a travel agency, offers a package insurance deal, this is no guarantee that the provisions will satisfy the authority. The details should always be sent in to the education office for their comments.

In this case a special insurance had to be negotiated which cost a little more per pupil. This is not, incidentally, the sort of extra cost which many parents will quibble about. They are usually healthily suspicious of the horrors of foreign parts and glad to see that every possible precaution is being taken.

Travel to and from Southampton was also a matter for negotiation. The company offers to arrange this through coach firms with which it is associated, but Smith found that he could make a better deal with the local firm which does all the travel business for his school and was therefore able to offer a very competitive rate, in addition to the service of known drivers operating from a garage just round the corner.

During the months preceding the trip, Smith sought out colleagues in other schools who had already been on educational cruises. He found that in every case the voyage had been a success.

He visited, for example, a junior school which had sent children to join one of the "mass booking" cruises operated by the local authority. For the sake of those contemplating such a trip with junior school children, some of the details which the young lady at this junior school gave to Smith might bear repetition.

The cruise was to Spain, Gibraltar and North Africa. The children were top class juniors (ten- and eleven-year-olds). They settled down quite well on board ship, although there was a fair amount of sea-sickness and some home-sickness which was associated, apparently at random, with either the arrival or non-arrival of letters. The two types of sickness together produced some fairly pathetic sights, and a teacher who can be, in a very real way, a substitute mother, capable of tucking children up in bed and holding their hands, is a necessity on a junior school cruising party.

The children faced the wonders of strange lands with aplomb. They liked Gibraltar best, because (to the chagrin of the idealists) it was " like England". The filth and despair in some of the Arab towns frightened them rather, and in Spain, the teacher discovered that even ten-year-old girls were not immune from the attentions of lusty youths.

They took to the different currencies without any trouble whatsoever, and thoroughly enjoyed bargaining with Arab traders, which they did with an authority and confidence rather disquieting to those who thought that we were bringing up a generation who no longer knew about Britannia ruling the waves.

It was not thought wise to give the children very much freedom while on shore, although they were by no means marched about in crocodiles. The teacher would indicate a street with shops and stalls and allow the children to work their way along it, while she walked up and down a couple of times and then waited at the other end for them to gather. Smith was planning to give his secondary children a little more freedom than this where appropriate.

Some of the junior boys, incidentally, bought small stuffed camels in Tangiers. They looked quite nice on the outside, but they turned out to be stuffed with some unspeakable material that was thoroughly infested with all sorts of creepy, leaping, biting livestock which came out looking for suitable nibbles as soon as things went quiet. In no time at all the camels were bobbing about in the wake of the ship, with their inhabitants presumably playing havoc with the unsuspecting fish.

Smith, his wife (a qualified teacher), two other colleagues (a man and a woman), and the party of children left school for Southampton a couple of days before the end of the autumn term and a week before Christmas. On the morning of departure, which was a Sunday, the voyagers were all present and correct except for one very unfortunate lad who had broken his collar bone in a school rugby game only the previous day. His teachers and parents had tried to persuade the hospital to fix him up so that he could go, and be attended by the ship's medical staff, but the hospital doctors played for caution and would not let him go. The boy was obviously bitterly disappointed, but there was some small consolation for his parents — they were very generously treated by the company with regard to the money which they had paid.

The journey to Southampton and the embarkation went without hitch and the cruise got under way. Back at home, parents looked with some apprehension at fearsome television weather charts which showed a great black mass of clustered isobars, and the reality at sea was in fact quite harrowing. For two or three days just about everyone except the ship's cat was horribly seasick. This, coupled with the fact that it was quite difficult to get to know the layout of the ship, made the early stages of the voyage rather confusing and a little miserable.

But things soon picked up. The rough seas were left behind, the climate warmed up, and the inexorable efficiency of the ship's staff, who each day produced a veritable mountain of paper giving instructions and information, worked to produce calm and order. Christmas morning was spent cruising gently among the Canary Islands in brilliant sunshine, with carols being sung on deck and the Christmas dinner being prepared down below.

The boys and girls were kept busy with a programme which divided the main part of each day into five periods, some of which were working periods in the classroom and others which were set aside for sport or voluntary activity. In the evenings there was usually a film and a discotheque. Older pupils were enrolled in a senior club and were given permission to go to bed a little later and to enjoy a little respite from the company of the younger ones.

The length of stay at the four ports of call varied from about twelve to thirty-six hours, and there was plenty of opportunity for guided tours, in addition to free time for exploring under the general supervision of teachers.

Having given this general outline, I propose to gather under headings some of the practical points which Smith discovered and which will be of value to other teachers contemplating educational cruising.

Supervision on Board

Teachers are responsible for their own parties. In practical terms this supervision starts when everyone is awakened at about seven-thirty, because although the teachers have their own cabin accommodation separate from the dormitories, it is necessary for them to go down to the dormitories to make sure that the

youngsters are in fact showing a leg. At the other end of the day, responsibility goes on until lights out at about nine-thirty. Ship's staff of course take charge of a lot of activities, administer meal arrangements and generally look after the dormitories at night but responsibility still bears upon the teachers all the time.

As a result, though the experience is enormously worthwhile and enjoyable, it should not be thought of just as a free holiday for the staff, especially if the minimum number of places for staff is taken up.

Supervision on Shore

When there was no guided tour, Smith divided up his party into
groups of five or six, each under a senior pupil who was responsible for counting them and keeping them together. These parties
were then sent off, after suitable briefing, and had to report back
at regular intervals. Dealing with this kept Smith and his colleagues
busy the whole time during shore excursions. All the children,
except for two or three more adventurous spirits, responded well
to these arrangements.

Girls needed particular care if they were to be guarded from the
attention of local youths. One girl in this party made the mistake
of smiling and winking at the wrong moment and was followed for
a whole day by no fewer than forty young men of all shapes and
sizes, a novelty which rapidly wore thin as the day went on.

Guided Coach Tours

These were good in terms of value and the view of the country
which they offered. But the guides themselves were a bit disappointing. They were not always clear speakers of English, and were
not educationists by any stretch of the imagination. Smith began
to weary of having the tourist facilities plugged and of being
shown an endless succession of new hotels, and had to stand up himself and interrupt in order to impart any geographical information.

The souvenir pedlars were annoyingly prominent on guided
tours. At one port of call there was a Marx Brothers type situation
whereby the same group of smiling highway robbers was in position and set up ready to start selling at every stop the coach made,
having dashed on ahead. The guides often appeared to have an
arrangement with local shopkeepers and took unnecessary toilet
stops near bazaars and groups of shops. One tour arrived back to
the ship an hour and a half late after a succession of such stops. In
the end Smith put his foot down at one place and caused some
arm-waving by refusing to allow the children to buy anything.

Money

The boys and girls did not take so well to foreign currency as
the junior school party mentioned earlier had done. They pre-

ferred to use English money, which was acceptable to traders in most tourist areas. There was a great and annoying tendency for the children to buy all sorts of rubbish at very high prices. Children on any sort of outing do this of course, but such is the

degree of potential extortion at cruise ports that teachers in charge would do well to give a little thought to how they are going to cope with it. It seems churlish to hold back a child's own money, but it might have to be done.

Spending money, an agreed amount for each child, decided collectively by the parents, was kept in the ship's bank, and Smith and his colleagues spent an hour or two before each port of call doing the necessary withdrawals and paper work.

Discipline

The boys and girls were very well behaved as a whole, although the mixing of parties with leaders whose standards differed from one another caused minor annoyances. Children could be and were punished by being sent to bed early, and there are now at

least two boys who have the distinction of having been caned on
the high seas, for repeatedly inconveniencing others by being late
at meeting points, and for bringing drink on board. A threat to

leave them on the ship when everyone went ashore came to naught
when the ship's staff refused the responsibility.

The constant degree of supervision which is needed means that
if the children are to have an enjoyable time without the feeling of
being nagged and restricted, then a very careful balance between
firmness and understanding must be struck and maintained
throughout the voyage.

The children did enjoy the cruise. They relished the utter
difference of it all; the experience of being in a closely organized

community at sea, and the contact with boys and girls from other schools. Clearly the educational gains were not simply in terms of seeing other lands and people, although these were real enough.

The staff found the cruise very tiring, but very worthwhile. This is clearly the sort of venture which needs to be in the charge of a very experienced and confident teacher, although colleagues new to the profession would have much to gain by going along as helpers. Although some free places are given, if other colleagues want to pay money and go, they should be welcomed with open arms.

The main operator of educational cruises in this country — indeed, so far as I can ascertain, the only such operator at the time of writing — is: British India Steam Navigation, P & O Building, Leadenhall Street, London E.C.3.

8
School Clubs and Societies

There are a lot of what might be termed small-scale out-of-school activities. I have in mind those school clubs and societies where boys and girls meet together once or twice a week to share a hobby or interest, without necessarily getting up to anything very earth-shaking, or making the pages of the Times Educational Supplement.

Some schools have a very large number of these — historical societies, for example, or debating societies, or stamp collecting clubs. In this chapter I will take a few examples and discuss them.

Stamp Collecting

I have a very soft spot for stamp collectors, for no very practical reason. It is simply that the thought of them brings to my mind a picture — in all probability totally without foundation in fact — of a more leisured age when people spent their evenings poring over leather-bound albums with magnifying glass and tweezers instead of throwing bottles at goalkeepers or watching bomb outrages on the television. It is not that I want children to be cut off from life, but I cannot help rejoicing quietly at the thought of them collecting stamps, or for that matter gazing at the stars or rushing about watching railway engines steam past.

Stamp collecting has had a strong upsurge in popularity in recent years, and the credit for this must go mainly to the policy of the Post Office. Those in charge have made strenuous efforts of late to co-operate with stamp enthusiasts.

I have seen this in the case of a colleague of mine who is always indulging in incomprehensible exercises which involve sending letters to village postmasters in remote parts of the country, and asking that they be sent back. The first time I saw him at this, I visualized a scene in a cluttered moorland post office, the oil lantern swinging and snow blowing under the door, and a be-whiskered individual saying: "Who do they'm think they be, Liza, expecting us to spend our time on such shennanagin with the squire's parcels not delivered, and half a day's muck-spreadin' still to do?"

I could not have been more wrong. It appears that trafficking of this sort, far from being the bane of postmasters' lives, is in fact what keeps them from going mad. They enter into it with zest, welcoming the respite from adding up Giro figures and steaming open unaddressed parcels of finnan haddock.

Most organized school stamp clubs are based in junior schools. Boys, particularly, of that age go through a collecting phase — they are likely to have trunkfuls of football programmes under their beds. Beer mats, cheese labels, cigarette cards, all have waxed and waned in popularity, together with the artificially stimulated advertising gimmick collections — football badges with petrol, for instance — but stamps have remained the aristocrats of collectable items. Because of this long-lasting popularity, the hobby of collecting them is very well documented, and it is very easy to find books and information on the subject.

Any teacher who is involved with a school stamp club or is thinking of starting one, could not really do better than read the booklet "Stamps in School" which is published by the Postal Publicity Branch of the Post Office. It covers the whole field, pointing out the social and educational advantages of children working together on their collections, and details of the sort of "spin off" which there might be in terms of art work, for instance, or outside visits. The booklet also details the various ways by which the Post Office provides services to collectors, and the material which is available for use in schools. The address to write to for this booklet is: The Schools Officer, Publicity Branch, Post Office Headquarters, St Martin's le Grand, London, EC1 A1 HQ.

War Games

Did I hear you say, "I beg your pardon"? So did I when I first heard of it. I was told about war games by a Welsh friend, a music teacher, who was approached by a senior boy at his school and asked if he would take charge of the school's war games society, the master who usually looked after it having left. At first he was rather taken aback, thinking that perhaps he would have to don a tin hat and gas mask and creep about in the undergrowth pretending to be wounded.

It transpired, however, that in reality, war games is the name given to the pastime of fighting battles with model soldiers and miniature military equipment, their movements being governed by an elaborate system of rules and scoring. It is apparently popular in a small number of schools, particularly ancient grammar schools where you are most likely to find boys of that endearingly twisted sort who are likely to become mixed up in this sort of thing.

The basis of the hobby is an interest in military models, their use in miniature battles being really just an extension of this. If you ever become mixed up in this activity, do not do what my friend did and start talking about "toy soldiers" will you? When he did this, he produced an effect worthy of a Bateman cartoon.

Railway Societies

This is another activity of the sort indulged in mainly by blasé fourteen year olds with IQs of over a hundred and twenty. The grammar school in the town where I work has quite an extensive enclave of lads who spend every minute of their spare time rushing off to remote map references to watch steam specials going past. These boys also like to attend those auction sales where they sell off old railway equipment. I know a parent who is forced to endure the presence in his home of signalling lamps, guards' caps and, stretching all the way up the stairs, a great long shunting pole.

It is interesting to see how, with the passing of steam, railway societies have developed a strong historico-nostalgic bias. There is a reluctance to accept that puffers have gone for ever, replaced by breaker-downers with diesel engines and things like clothes horses for scraping electricity off overhead wires.

Model Aeroplanes

Aero-modelling is a branch of the larger world of model engineering, but has the advantage that it can be taken to a quite advanced level without any actual engineering taking place. If the model planes are to get off the ground, they need to be light and are thus not turned on lathes or welded with oxy-acetylene gear, but constructed from bits of wood stuck together with balsa cement. This is why aero-modelling is more suitable for schools and for the supervision of non-specialist teachers than is model boating or the construction of miniature traction engines.

The materials are quite cheap and results very satisfying, with aeroplanes actually swooping around the sky in all directions. A boy who makes a flying model cannot help but gain a fairly comprehensive empirical knowledge of the physical laws which govern flight. I always remember with some pride the moment, as a pupil, I realized in a physics lesson that I knew more about elementary aero-dynamics than did the rather inexperienced teacher who was trying to explain it to us.

A model aeroplane club was formed in a school in the North of England as a result of interest among the boys. They put a little pressure on the hierarchy of the school and were found a small room in which to build their models and hold their meetings. This was supposed to take place under the very general supervision of the woodwork master because model aircraft are basically made of wood (the fact that he did not know a fuselage from a Mae West was not considered of consequence). I have to record, though, that in this particular case, few models were actually built on the premises. It seemed to me that half-built ones were brought from home and left conspicuously about the place to impress authority while the members spent their time in gentlemanly conversation and crafty smoking. Every now and again, when the pressure was on and the authorities seemed to be closing in, the boys put on a very impressive exhibition which always brought fulsome praise from the headmaster and fanned the impotent rage of the members of staff who were trying to have the club closed down as a hotbed of vice and intrigue.

All these boys needed was a little more interest shown by their teachers. Theirs was an example of the rare type of school club which functions with very little staff help or involvement.

Debating

Formal debating societies in schools are usually formed by
teachers who have acquired a taste for debating while at univer-
sity. I visited a school which has a debate in the library every
Monday lunchtime, and I know there are many more which have
regular meetings. In this school the subjects are chosen by a committee of pupils from among suggestions left in a box by any
member of the school.

The most difficult thing about a debating society is for the
staff to restrain themselves from too much intervention both in
the selection of debating subjects and in the debates themselves.
Staff suggestions about the selection of subjects ought really to
be confined to advice about their sheer practicability — whether
there is enough controversy involved, for instance, or whether
anyone is likely to have the necessary specialized knowledge. To
go further than this and to try to dictate policy on the basis of
purely adult criteria is to invite withdrawal of interest.

In the same way, the adults have to contain themselves during
the actual debates. It takes a great deal of self-control to allow the
children to go on with their immature and occasionally absurd
arguments when it seems that a word or two might help to
straighten things out. Such interruptions should though, be kept
to an absolute minimum, because the children will inevitably
resent what they see as muscling in by members of staff on what
is perhaps the only occasion when pupils have the opportunity of
airing their thoughts unimpeded by the framework of the classroom situation. Neither do the youngsters take kindly to being
treated patronizingly by adult debaters. In short, it is best to let
them get on with it. We all of us had immature ideas once and we
grew out of them naturally, rather than as a result of adult
promptings.

The lunchtime debating society which I mentioned earlier
follows the full formal rules of debating. I am never sure of the
wisdom of this but teachers who know more about it than I do
always cry me down when I express any doubt. It is simply that
I am doubtful about the value of too much formality among
exuberant adolescents who have plenty to say and yet who have
not grown to relish procedure and formality for their own sake. I

am also thinking of the fact that many of these youngsters will find themselves doing their adult debating not in formal debating clubs, but on the committees of organizations which are too often almost completely bogged down with procedural rules. Union committee meetings, for example, have to be experienced to be believed. I cannot help thinking that we ought to be trying to encourage our boys and girls away from this sort of thing rather than fostering it.

Still, this is carping. The debating societies do at least make the boys and girls talk and argue along directed lines, and the application of formal rules clearly worked well in the society which I saw. Certainly it is necessary to work within the rules if competitive debating is ever envisaged with neighbouring schools or in one of the national debating competitions.

Half the battle is probably to have a good chairman. The one I visited had in this position a fifth form girl of sardonic wit, forceful personality and total unflappability.

Bridge

In many school staff-rooms at lunchtime you will find a gentle-manly game of bridge in progress, cigar smoke perhaps adding to the generally civilized air which those who indulge in the game tend to promote around themselves. The only disadvantage is that if there is only one staff-room, the presence of a concentrated game of bridge, with its usual accompaniment of calls for silence, can bring about arguments and clashes of personality. The solution is perhaps to take the game out of the staff-room at least once or twice a week and involve some of the pupils. This has happened at one comprehensive school which I know, where a few keen pupils are learning to play the game at least to the level where it is a pleasant pastime and a social asset. In time they will look around for competition, but this is by no means the main object of the exercise.

Chess

It cannot be said too often that this is a young person's game. This is not to say that older folk cannot enjoy it, for this would be palpable nonsense, but it is a fact that youngsters between the ages of eleven and seventeen learn the game faster than adults and, having done so, play more aggressively and with more success, than their elders, at least at the level of most amateurs. It is a chastening experience, and one which many teachers who look after chess clubs have gone through, to teach a boy the basic moves and then to find oneself being beaten by him only a matter of weeks later.

The only reservation I have about chess is that it is not really a very social game. I once played league chess, and every Tuesday night I went and pored over boards in various parts of the town for two or three hours at a time. During the whole of that time I hardly exchanged two words with any of my oppenents, and I have no recollection now of the names of any of my team mates.

It is noticeable that the game is very popular in junior schools. Some towns and counties have a regular schools congress during the holidays or at weekends and the sight of so many very youthful competitors in deep concentration is very warming.

Small Bore Rifle Shooting

This started in public schools and was basically connected with school cadet forces. But there is now a growing tendency for schools in the state system to take up the sport as such, devoid of any military connections. In recognition of this, the controlling schools organization has changed its name from the Public Schools Small Bore Rifle Association to the British Schools Small Bore Rifle Association.

There seems little doubt that any school which takes up small bore shooting has no difficulty whatsoever in interesting boys and girls in the activity, and that any teacher who introduced it would, in all probability, be able to capture the imagination of some youngsters who were not particularly bothered about other forms of out-of-school activity.

The main snag is the provision of a range, which would be really too expensive for any state school to provide for itself from scratch. There may be the possibility of using the range belonging to a nearby club, however. Guns cost about £50 each for worthwhile new ones, but the cost might be brought down by buying second-hand. Those who run the sport in schools point out that youngsters learn a great deal about concentration and about muscular relaxation from shooting, qualities which are not found in other sports and activities.

Competitive shooting is usually done by post, and because of this is very conveniently arranged and devoid of travelling difficulties. Over a hundred schools compete each year in the BSSRA's postal league.

It goes without saying that you do not introduce shooting into a school without first taking proper advice, which is easily available either from the BSSRA or the National Small Bore Rifle Association, which is the adult body. Among other things, they will advise about equipment and the design of ranges. The police will also wish to know about any range which is opened and about the security of weapons which are stored at the school.

There is criticism about teaching boys or girls to shoot. This is a matter for the conscience of the individual teacher or headmaster, but the defenders of the sport point out that many of the shooting accidents which take place through youngsters mishandling air guns or shotguns would be avoided if they had been taught the proper handling of firearms. It is certainly true that those of us who were taught to shoot in the forces have inherited a very healthy respect for guns, to the extent that we even feel a little uncomfortable about our small sons pointing toy revolvers at us.

Archery

This is another of those activities where the problem is not so much to arouse interest as to find enough space and equipment to provide experience for a reasonable number of boys and girls. The provision of facilities is not such a problem as with rifle shooting however, and the qualities which it requires are very similar. Because of the existence of school playing fields, in fact, the school archery club might well find that it has an advantage over the adult group, which often has trouble in finding space within which it can both shoot and operate the stringent safety regulations which are obviously needed.

Quite obviously, the establishment of archery also needs specialist advice, and in this case the organization to go to is the Association for Archery in Schools. The Grand National Archery

Association also operates a scheme by which teachers can gain proficiency certificates for teaching archery to young people.

There is a postal competition run by the AAS, organized so that the required rounds can be shot during a normal lunch-hour.

I feel that the great strength of both rifle shooting and archery lies in the fact that they bring the boys and girls who practise them into a situation where it is very necessary to concentrate, not only in order to achieve worthwhile results but also to avoid breaches of the safety regulations. In both cases the necessity for such concentration is instantly obvious. It is not necessary, for instance, to preach to a boy that if he points his rifle in the wrong direction he might drill a hole in someone. In the same way a lapse of concentration while squeezing the trigger or drawing a bow will clearly show itself on the target score.

Thus the teacher is put in the position of asking for a high standard of self-discipline and concentration not for reasons which are vague or "because I say so" but which are very simply and obviously understood.

The same quality is found in some outdoor activities — it is easy to see why you rope up on a rock face for instance, or wear a life-jacket in a canoe — but the point is that shooting can be done in school. What I am really saying is that archery and shooting offer a means of bringing boys and girls, while still on their school premises, into contact with something exciting and obviously potentially lethal, being rendered safe only because of the rules and safeguards which have to be observed. For these reasons I feel that more schools should consider taking them up.

It is worth finally noting, on the subject of archery particularly, that it is a good example of a healthy outdoor sport which can be enjoyed by youngsters with physical handicaps of one sort or another, or who have simply not the sort of co-ordination which is necessary for a ball game.

9

Fund-raising and Community Service

There are those who feel that out-of-school activities ought always to produce some social benefit for others. Money ought to be raised for charity, for example, or there should be garden digging and wall-papering in old folks' bungalows. It is said that other forms of activity are too introverted, and that in the out-of-school field every opportunity should be sought to help the children look outwards.

This is a point of view which has many virtues. I do feel, though, that social service is not the only aim. It is equally idealistic and desirable to teach children that there are some things in life which are worth doing purely for their own sake without any utilitarian motive. This is something which tends to be forgotten in our materialistic world. We are quick to point out that selfishness is not enough and that human beings should help each other, but we somehow overlook the very real need, which we all have, to do something difficult and useless. We see the sublimation of this need in those girls who want to know why they have to take history when they are going to be typists, or in parents who write in wanting to know why Johnny is wasting his time on trombone lessons when he is going to be a sheet metal worker.

In this sort of environment, it is a major and laudable achievement to interest a teenager in an activity which is sophisticated, difficult and of no earthly use. It is the children who collect stamps and look through telescopes who are the hope of our race rather than those who hold jumble sales for the mentally handicapped, or go on sponsored walks.

Having said that I must rush on, before lynching parties arrive from various social and charitable organizations, and state that of course socially conscious activities are good and desirable for children. I am only making a plea here of rebellion against the point of view that *all* activities must produce some social benefit.

It is obviously fitting that the natural impulsive generosity which most children have should be organized and directed, and that they should be made aware of the areas of need and difficulty in our world. This being so, there are a number of points worthy of consideration.

The main effort in most schools in the direction of charitable and social work consists of raising money. Money is very useful, in spite of the fact that it may well be less rewarding education-ally for children to spend time and energy raising it, than it would be for them actually to go out and work among people who are less fortunate than themselves. Many schools spend at least a part of their energies on supporting a favourite charity. Head teachers find that they have to select very carefully those appeals which they pass on to the children, because they are inundated through-out the year with brochures and letters urging the merits of this or that charity.

One Fund-raising Effort

Here is an example of how one school helped one particular charity. A house-master in a large school asked his children if they would try, over a period of time, to raise enough money to buy a guide dog for a blind person, through the Guide Dogs Association. He felt this to be a very suitable sort of aim for a school. It combined a lot of the appeal which animals have for children, with the virtue of being a human rather than an animal charity. Animals do quite well on the whole in the competition for donated money, and schools are better employed in pointing out to children the areas of human need which exist. Supporting the Guide Dogs for the Blind Association also has the advantage that if enough money is raised, then the donors can choose the name of an actual dog and have a picture of it. There is therefore the feeling of working towards something real and attainable, rather than merely throwing money down any anonymous chute to join piles of other loot given by lots of other people.

There was never much sense of urgency about this campaign. It was the house-master's idea to run the appeal gently but continuously, allowing the money to build up slowly and steadily over perhaps two or three years.

The opening shot was to have been a sponsored long-distance march — this was when the sponsored walk was a new and exciting idea. There was going to be a relay march to the coast, the school bus crawling through the night stuffed with sleeping walkers. It never happened though. There was a distinct lack of enthusiasm for the project on the part of the local education authority. Their position in such matters is that they have to be informed, and even though they are not really empowered to place a ban on such an activity happening, as was planned, well outside school hours, it does not really do to go against their wishes.

The house-master and his colleagues decided to replace the ill-fated march with a sort of sponsored map-reading exercise. They all went off up to Cannock Chase, a large tract of moorland and forest in North Staffordshire which offers the possibility of walking fairly long distances without coming into conflict with heavy traffic. This removed the principal objection of the education authority. The idea of the exercise was that various members of the house-staff loafed about on the Chase in the sunshine acting as check points, while the boys and girls marched all over the place with maps in their hands trying to find the route which would allow visiting all the check points in the shortest possible time. They were sponsored according to the number of check points they managed to visit.

They also carried collecting tins to wave under the noses of unsuspecting picnickers and courting couples who were flushed from the undergrowth. For this part of the scheme, a street collection licence was needed, and it was granted on application to the chief constable. There seemed to be no difficulty about this; it is apparently a matter only of regulating the number of collections which take place in a given area over a period of time.

The weather was good and everyone had a lot of fun. The only moment of anxiety came when the house-master, studying the

map in the shade of the school bus, was suddenly galvanized by
the fact that in very small print in the area where the walking was
going on were the words "Rifle Range". No one, though, was
bullet-riddled. Everyone got tired, a few romances were struck
up among the youngsters, and a fair amount of money was raised.

Sponsored Events

Later on there was a sponsored swim, involving house-staff again,
as well as the pupils. One of the teachers, a physical educationist

and an Olympic medal-winning athlete of some repute, demonstrated that prowess on the track is no guarantee of proficiency
in the water, and spent the evening lashing the water to foam to
no visible effect and calling down all sorts of unmentionable
retribution on the head of whoever thought of the idea.

It is probably a good idea to place an upper limit of the number
of lengths of the bath, or the number of miles walked or whatever,
so that not only is the amount of money to be given by each
person kept within bounds, but children are prevented from over-
reaching themselves in their enthusiasm.

More than one school has run what seems to me the ultimate
sponsored activity — a sponsored silence. The boys and girls

gather in the hall or a classroom and keep their peace for an agreed period of time, being sponsored in the usual way at so much a minute. It is apparently very popular and successful.

One trouble with these sponsored things is accounting for the money. The usual way of operating them is to give each participant a form which he takes along to people asking them to sign up as a pledge of being willing to give so much per mile, or length of the pool, or whatever. The exercise completed, he has his form certificated by the organizer and goes along to the signatories to collect the cash. Unfortunately there are always some who will not pay up. It is always advisable, in fact, to talk to the participants and try to convince them that it is better to be selective about their sponsors, choosing those who are considered likely to honour their commitments, rather than gathering an impressively long list of people who have signed while drunk or merely in avuncular mood, and who will retreat over the horizon when approached for the actual gold. This sort of thing, if it happens to younger children, can severely shake their faith in human nature. Some organizations, such as, I believe, the National Heart Foundation, take it upon themselves to approach defaulters after the forms have been handed in, but I doubt the sheer practicality of this.

Sometimes the participants themselves are at least partly to blame. In a sponsored swim which I heard of, there was a little girl who had estimated that her limit was likely to be about four lengths, and who had collected promises on that basis. In the actual swim, though, she was so carried away by the excitement that she breasted the waves to the tune of no fewer than thirty lengths. As a result, the school was besieged by horrified mums whose children had arrived home in tears because they were in debt to the tune of several quid each.

The effect of all this is that even with total honesty on the part of the participants there will be discrepancies between the amount shown on each sponsorship form and the amount actually paid in. This makes it difficult, if not impossible, to eliminate any possibility of sharp practice. It is necessary to be realistic about this. If there are large numbers of children handling quite considerable sums of money which are difficult to account for precisely, then it is likely rather than otherwise that one or two of them will line their pockets a bit. This is something which can spread through a group very quickly. I am quite sure that in the large-scale sponsored walks, and for that matter the flag days and street collections which national charitable organizations run, there is quite certain to be a bit of fiddling. It may be that some of the walkers and collectors only join in because of the pickings to be had. This is highly cynical talk, but I am convinced that these things do go on.

There may well be absolutely foolproof methods of running sponsored events, and many of us would like to hear what they are. I mention the snags only in order to draw attention to them.

Precautions

Safety and first-aid arrangements are important for any of these sponsored walks and swims. Walking on main roads is best avoided, for it has been shown that even the best regulated road events are accident-prone. Today's motorists assume the right to hurtle around the place without considering the possibility of coming upon people doing such an outlandish thing as walking, and it is worth trying very hard to find a course which is removed from traffic. Cannock Chase, already mentioned, is ideal for schools within reach, being an area of moorland — but not wild and remote moorland — criss-crossed by paths and tracks. Large parks offer a possibility, and the grounds of stately homes can sometimes be made available after negotiation.

First-aid arrangements should be looked after by someone who knows all about it. For a large event, the St John's Ambulance Brigade can be approached. In any case, thought must be given to setting up places where blistered walkers can be helped, and there must be adequate transport available for those who can walk no further or who need to be taken home or to hospital.

It is always best to talk to the police about any outdoor sponsored event. Even if they decide that it is too small to warrant any special arrangements by them, it can do no harm to discuss it; they have a great deal of experience to draw on which may well be of help, and they have the knack of thinking up snags which you had never dreamed of.

The overall guiding principle for a teacher running any charity event of this nature is that he should seek the guidance of the appropriate experts in each field. It is only the work of a few minutes to get on the phone to the police or the local St John's and yet an amazing number of people never do this, preferring to proceed in their own way, sometimes with unfortunate or even tragic results.

Collecting Things

Silver paper is another popular fund-raiser. It is traditionally used by those collecting for guide dogs because the Guide Dogs for the Blind Association have encouraged it for a long time, although they no longer handle its collection and disposal themselves. Collecting silver paper is not without its snags; it is bulky in relation to value and takes up a lot of storage space. Not all silver paper is saleable, apparently, and to be on the safe side it is better to stick to that which is unequivocally aluminium foil — cooking foil, for instance, and the food containers used for frozen foods and take-away Chinese meals.

Some schools have raised money by collecting newspaper and selling it to waste paper merchants, but the imagination boggles a bit at the thought of the amount of space needed to store enough to make a practical sum. A modern school building has hardly enough storage place for the spare toilet rolls let alone room to put the several tons of used newspaper which are needed to make up a useful amount.

Jumble Sales and Fêtes

Children really enjoy the more traditional fund-raising activities, like jumble-sales and garden fêtes. A jumble-sale can be fun and can teach the children an enormous amount, even if it is only that there are some very rapacious and dishonest people about. Some of the more professional jumble-sale attenders need watching; they appear with huge shopping-bags into which disappears everything

within range, whether nominally for sale or not. The room where
the sale is to be held should be absolutely bare of all movable
objects which are not involved, otherwise you will have to chase
after great matrons carrying window poles and blackboards.

Collecting jumble can also take the children on an interesting
door to door tour of the neighbourhood and before long they
will invariably find some lonely old lady who will have them all
in for cups of tea, while Sir waits patiently down the road in the
school bus.

Those who organize jumble-sales would do well to remember
that quality is a better aim than quantity when gathering in the
stuff. I have seen too many jumble-sales have only moderate
success because of this. The tendency which exists for jumble-
sales to be used as an alternative to the dustbin should be firmly
resisted.

I once taught in a school which had jumble-sales, and one old
lady, who meant very well, always seemed to have us busy for
hours at a time staggering to and fro with festering piles of ancient
books and great rusty iron objects the purpose of which had long
been forgotten.

When collecting, the best thing is to head for good-class hous-
ing estates where, with any luck, there will be a good haul of
baby clothes and children's cast off garments.

A garden fête can be a good money-spinner and the children
will enjoy both the organization and the event itself, especially
if there is one of those stalls where the staff take it in turns to
stick their heads through a board and have wet sponges thrown
at them for three pence a time. The last time I did this (it was
also the first) I realized with mounting horror that the sponges
were extemely heavy and, when hurled by the lustier members of
the first fifteen, were arriving with what seemed like lethal force,
hitting the board alongside my head with a thump and rattle akin
to that produced by an 88 mm shell. My colleague and fellow
target caused something of a diversion, however, by so arranging
his arms that he was able to catch the missiles and fling them back
into the crowd, to the consternation of the distinguished guests
who were touring the attractions at the time.

A fair, or fête, call it what you like (a head I know would not use the word fête because he was sated with jokes about "A Fête Worse Than Death"), can include almost anything you care to name: whelk stalls, guess the deputy head's weight, local footballers selling autographs, a hot dog stall and so forth.

The best money-spinners are probably bottle stalls and tombola stalls. The usual way of running a bottle stall is to sell tickets at a flat rate, which are exchanged for a bottle bearing the matching number. It might be a bottle of perfume or tomato ketchup or perhaps a bottle of Scotch. It is necessary to have a generous number of expensive prizes displayed in a prominent position.

Donkeys will probably make a loss against their hiring fee, but they bring the kids in and, what is not often realized, they keep the children occupied while their mums and dads spend money around the stalls.

What is absolutely essential at one of these affairs is amplifying equipment which will play endless pop music at such volume that one has to brace oneself against being thrown bodily to the ground by the sheer force of the sound. Anything else can be hacked up or made in school, but for the sound equipment, professional hire is the only adequate answer.

Other Ideas

There are all sorts of minor fund-raising devices which I have seen tried and tested. Some of the children in my charge once washed cars on a Saturday when their owners, the staff of the school, were in for the day rehearsing a play. This proved to be rather slow and relatively unrewarding. Some of the staff were, in fact, mildly put out at the idea of having forked out 20p for the privilege of having their cars rendered several degrees dirtier than they were before. Neither did it do the boys and girls much good to get themselves soaked to the skin in a raw November day, and it was with some relief that I counted them all present and breathing freely the following Monday morning.

Then there was the time I took some children and staff out carol-singing for charity, a day or two before Christmas. We presented a fairly traditional appearance, with a lantern on a pole and the more cherubic youngsters well to the fore.

One of the boys was walking on crutches right up to the day of the expedition, and I was rubbing my hands with glee at the thought of propelling him before us up the drives of affluent suburbanites, hopping and swinging along and touching his cap like Tiny Tim. "Not a dry eye in the place!" we kept telling each

other. Unfortunately, though, he went and had the plaster off in spite of all our pleadings.

Still, we looked quite professional which, in a sense, made the shock of our singing all the more traumatic. Time after time we had the experience of seeing dinner-jacketed executives call their wives to the door ("Quickly, darling, the Waits!") and stand there wreathed in Corona smoke, looking every inch of £8,000 a year, only to blink in a bewildered fashion at the cacophonous sounds which we produced. Still, they forked out.

At one staggeringly large house, of the kind which we point out to children in social history books as examples of something now extinct, I was called in to take the collecting box round the guests at a party. I passed sheepishly around, blinking in the reflected light from all the jewellery and trying to hide the hole in the seat of my trousers. (Some teachers have drinking trousers, I have singing trousers.) "What price professional status now, I thought!"

The latest fund-raising device of which I have heard consists of drawing out whatever funds are already in, and investing them in stocks and shares. At least one school has made an enormous success of this. The problem is that there is, of course, a chance of losing. This might be all very well in the sense that the educational gains might compensate for financial losses, but looked at purely in terms of raising money, the risk might seem too high.

The investment idea can, though, be used in less ambitious ways. One house-master, for instance, gave £5 to each of his eleven tutorial groups and instructed them to use the money in such a way as to double it if at all possible. Few limits were made, although a hope was expressed that resourcefulness would pass beyond the point of nipping down to the betting shop to get the fiver on a strongly-fancied treble.

What actually happened was that most of the groups used their money to buy raffle prizes, or materials to make soft toys and sweets which they could sell. One interesting raffle had as its prizes a series of "Slave Girls". These were senior young ladies who gave their services for the day to the winners. The teachers tried not to enquire too deeply into all the things they were expected to do, although the first one was lucky enough to be won by the senior mistress. The poor girl spent the day running about in all directions and rapidly lost many illusions about the easy life which senior members of staff are commonly supposed to lead. Another of these £5 investment groups bought a quantity of shoe-cleaning materials and set up shop outside the staff-room where they fixedly gazed at the shabby brogues of the gentlemen of the staff as they passed in and out.

Clearly there is almost no limit to the number of fund-raising ideas which can be dreamed up and used, but it is important to

keep in proportion the amount of time which is spent on such
ventures by staff and children. It is too easy to assume that time
is free, whereas in fact the time of a busy teacher is valuable, and
it is important to make sure that it is used to the best advantage.

Direct Social Service

Fund-raising is all very well, but it is obviously true that there is
great educational benefit to be gained from allowing children to
do their good works in person. They can do so many things, and
one constantly hears of boys and girls of secondary school age re-
decorating or cleaning old people's houses, or helping out at the
local day nursery.

In fact, of course, this sort of thing is seen as so essential to the
development of young adolescents that a great deal of it is outside
the scope of this book, because it is done not as an out-of-school
activity but as part of the school course. This is particularly so in
those schools which have a special outward looking course for the
boys and girls in the upper part of the school who are not preparing for external examinations.

A teacher who finds himself, though, in a school which has no
contact with the local community might feel that one good way
to start is to try helping the local old people. The need always
exists for such assistance, but it is important to remember one
thing. Help will only be welcomed if it is of real value, and preferably if it continues in some regular way. Those who have the
professional care of old people, or of pre-school children for that
matter, do not welcome well-meaning dabblers with very much
enthusiasm. At the bottom of all such welfare work is a foundation of unsentimental hard graft — and if the children learn this,
then one of the aims of doing such work will have been achieved.

Most towns have some sort of Old People's Welfare Committee
which may have some connection with the local council — in any
event, the information department of the council will know how
to get in touch with them. The best way to start such social work
is to talk it over with someone from such a committee, with a
view to finding some well-defined specific tasks which your
children can undertake for a start — fetching in coal, doing

shopping and so on. It is necessary, I think, to grow from small beginnings, because it will be disappointing for everyone if grandiose plans are made and come to nothing.

Local old people should not be forgotten either when school plays and concerts are being organized. It is often possible to offer them free seats and to organize transport for some of them by coach or school bus.

10
Older Pupils

Now that the school leaving age is sixteen, and a large proportion of our pupils are in any case staying on beyond that age, the question arises of how we can think of ways in which out-of-school activities can be made to appeal to boys and girls who are in fact young adults.

A boy or girl who is old enough to get married, to vote or leave home is less likely than his more junior colleagues to be attracted by the idea of staying behind after school to blow a flugel horn or to stick stamps in a book. This is not, I hasten to add, to say that they should not do these things or that they never do them. It is a matter of facing the facts. The fifth- and sixth-former is a harder nut to crack than is a second-former.

In some cases the nut-cracking might be unnecessary, as some older pupils find their own out-of-school activities, preferring to leave school, with its restrictions and uniforms, behind at four o'clock. I knew of a seventh-year boy in a comprehensive school who was regarded for some time by his teachers as being rather quiet, and on the face of it reluctant to take part in the community life of the school.

It was only by chance that the staff discovered that this boy was in fact very active in a local youth organization of the type which spends its time taking under-privileged children on camps and outings. Large chunks of his spare time were occupied in the supervision of such ventures. To suggest that this boy was in some way unworthy because he gave little time to the school outside of his lessons would clearly be unjust, and yet his very reticence was liable to lead to this mistake being made. I must add that there was in his case the special circumstance of having come late to the school, with his social service activities already developed. He presumably felt it unnecessary to say anything about them, or to use the school for anything other than purely scholastic purposes.

There are two aspects to the question of participation by senior pupils in out-of-school activities. On the one hand it is desirable that they should take a leading part in those activities which are designed to involve all or most of the age groups within the school, for older students have much to offer, not least in their ability to take responsibility and to lessen the burden on staff.

In many cases, such youngsters are superior to their teachers in some areas, a state of affairs which every teacher of sixteen to eighteen-year-olds has to come to terms with. In my own choir, for instance, the girls are clearly dissatisfied with my standard of organization and tidiness, and spend a lot of time clearing up music after me and dropping thinly veiled hints about inefficiency and squalor. The school brass band which I know has, as another example, at least one senior member who can and does take a full band practice when the bandmaster is unable to attend.

Keeping the interest of boys and girls when they become seniors is not, however, as I hinted earlier, an easy matter. The sixth-forms of our schools are littered with ex-recorder players, ex-actors and ex-sports stars. It is almost as if they are easing themselves pain-lessly one step at a time out of school into the outside world during the three years before they actually leave.

I have no glib answer to this. The pressure of examination work clearly has a great deal to do with the problem. Even where it would be clearly possible, given a little commonsense and organiza-tion of time, for a pupil to carry on with his or her interests, there is often panic, and everything is given up in the interests of study. Sometimes pressure is brought to bear by parents who are anxious for solid academic achievement, and who see recorder-tootling and netball as obstacles to ultimate success. At other times the pressure comes from academically-minded teachers who also feel that examination attainment is all-important. Such feelings on the part of ambitious parents are perhaps understandable, but fellow teachers, one feels, ought to know better.

It may well be that when a senior pupil is counselled about his courses and examination entries and his timetable is put together at the beginning of the year, that his out-of-school activities should be included in the discussion, on equal terms with his academic subjects, so that he can be encouraged to do at least something other than his lessons. This is surely necessary for any pupil who wants to preserve his sanity.

This is not to suggest that he should actually be coerced into taking part in debating or swimming or whatever, but that the importance of such activities be pointed out, and the suggestion

made that the idea of giving up everything would bear a closer examination. It might be that in the course of this counselling, some boys and girls would need to be told to cut down a little on what they are doing, although it is generally true that the pupils who do everything and who are seen organizing every activity in sight are usually the ones who are at the top of the list when the A-level results come out.

It is an advantage to all if younger and older pupils can mix together and learn from each other in the out-of-school setting. A fine picture comes into minds here to cherubic youngsters struggling with their woodwork or crocheting, while large and benign sixth-formers pass among them offering kindly advice, like Old Brook in *Tom Brown's Schooldays*.

Alas, though, while it would not do at all to say that this sort of thing never happens — I could give many examples from my own experience — it would be less than the truth to suggest that it is the normal pattern of events. Indeed, to expect this sort of thing too much and too often is to stretch the tolerance of senior pupils a little. They need to be allowed to go at their own pace and in their own way. The interesting thing is that there are teachers who do not realize this. They expect their seniors to attend and to give their time and experience freely, and it never enters their heads that some resentment might be piling up. It is very possible for willing sixth-formers to be put on beyond the point of reason. We really have no right to demand too much from them in the way of example-setting and help for younger members. We are the teachers after all.

Thus the second aspect of out-of-school activities for senior pupils begins to emerge. Some activities need to be laid on which are expressly designed for the seniors and which free them from the burden of having to look after younger children or having to accept restrictions which, while appropriate for juniors, are superfluous for sixteen- to eighteen-year-olds.

The provision of activities which give the opportunity for relaxation in a fairly free atmosphere might well keep youngsters from going off and joining in less desirable goings-on.

A Social Evening

In order to meet this sort of requirement, some schools run a sixth-form social evening at regular intervals, perhaps once a week or once a month. It seems that the most successful of these are the ones in which the staff do very little other than provide the use of the school and its equipment, and take it in turns to give the minimum supervision which is required by law. This usually takes the form of a teacher sitting in the staff room catching up on some marking, and every now and again walking round to make sure that nothing is set on fire and that no babies are actually conceived on the premises, an event which is not catered for in most school insurance schemes.

If the teachers try to organize things too much, the boys and girls will often just stop coming. They have enough of organization by adults during the day, and it is not surprising that any attempt at its imposition after school, however well meant, will result in their voting with their feet. It is worth remembering this even when it becomes clear that the boys and girls are a bit short of ideas, and that nothing ever seems to go on but desultory billiards and half-hearted table tennis, played to the accompaniment of devastatingly loud pop records.

This dilemma is exactly that which is found in most youth clubs. Any youth leader will tell you of the frustration of dealing with

youngsters who have no wish to organize themselves and yet who resist any attempt by adults to help.

In the case of our sixth-form social evening, we can have a clear conscience, I feel. The boys and girls work hard at their studies and we should be content with their somewhat apathetic "entertainments" without feeling the need to continue by night the relentless improvement of their minds which we pursue during the school day.

What the supervising teacher can perhaps do is to use the sixth-form social evening to make the acquaintance of any senior pupils whom he does not see very often, particularly those who are influential among their fellows. This can perhaps be achieved by strolling up and joining in a game of snooker, but not too much success should be expected. The walls are often up on these occasions and one thing which teenagers resent is any attempt by adults to patronize or be "one of the boys". The only time this is even moderately acceptable is when the adult concerned is obviously young enough to be counted among the faithful.

The freedom which is given to sixth-formers on these occasions should not be stretched to the point where they are allowed to abuse the school's equipment. This they will surely do sooner or later if some restrictions are not imposed. The certain way to lose valuable basket-balls or to have long-cherished film projectors and tape-recorders converted into masses of twisted and smoking metal is to allow them to be used by the seniors without check or super-vision. The best way to handle this is to place one of them in absolute charge and make him responsible for any loss or damage, even unto bankruptcy or death itself. If a suitably fearsome rugby player is chosen for this task, or better still a large girl who is on the threshold of a career as a physical education teacher, every-thing should be fine.

The Discotheque

A word now about discotheques. I deal with them here because it is not possible to mix with senior pupils for long without coming face to face or at least eardrum to eardrum with this phenomenon of musico-technological achievement. The boys and girls like to have discotheque evenings not only for their own sake but because they are very good fund-raisers. Children will fork out large sums to attend them, and once inside they will continue to pay large sums for the privilege of drinking warm Coca-Cola.

A disco though, in spite of what I have said about freedom, needs firm staff supervision. This is mainly because it will act as a magnet to all the local youngsters. They will flock along on unstable looking motor cycles hoping to be allowed in, and among them will always be a proportion who come with the intention of wresting loose all the cloakroom fittings, or of starting very dramatic incidents involving the brandishing of knives and the use of out-dated Hollywood jargon.

Because of all this, if the boys and girls want to hold a disco-theque for which tickets are to be sold, then even though the organization can be in their hands it is very necessary that staff supervision be available. Any teacher who is asked to provide this supervision should find as many colleagues as he can to help him.

The most important requirement for a discotheque is that a lot of the very latest and most popular records should be played as loudly as possible. The mistake should not be made of thinking that this means the records which are in the hit parade. Urban teenagers have a pop music culture all their own which often seems to bear little relation to the official one as purveyed by BBC Radio One. The best way of coping with this is to engage a professional who runs a mobile disco. It might be that one of the pupils in the school has a relative who does this sort of thing, or one of the old boys may be demonstrating the irrelevance of his A-levels by making several thousand a year at it. A contact of this sort might result in the organization having to pay a reduced fee. This would be very worthwhile, as these gentlemen do tend to-wards the expensive. A good disc jockey makes the sort of fee which in my day had to be spread among lots of chaps in gold tuxedos bobbing up and down in serried ranks playing trumpets and saxophones. The old joke about being a skilled player of the gramophone has come true with a vengeance.

On the night of the disco the disc jockey, who will bear some improbable pseudonym like Hiram Gazebo or Bunter Pebblebed will arrive in an ancient van with illegal tyres and will carry into the hall enough electronic equipment to furnish the Pentagon War Room. It is essential therefore, that electrical plugs of some sort are available, although if the chap is worth his fee he will have enough cable, plugs and bits and pieces to conjure electricity from somewhere. During the performance he stands behind a sort of electric powered managing director's desk, wearing earphones and pressing buttons which cause lights to flash and the sound to become relentlessly louder. The decibel level is totally indescrib-able and is such as to cause annoyance to aircraft flying overhead.

The best place for most of the supervising staff is outside in the

foyer. Every now and again, by turn, one of them can enter the
holocaust and patrol round making sure that mayhem, rape and
arson are not overtly taking place. Sometimes younger colleagues
prove the value of a modern liberal education by actually taking
part in the dancing.

The cloakrooms at a discotheque, or indeed at any form of
dance, need careful security arrangements. A police officer informs
me that there are people who attend dances with the sole intention of stealing coats and other belongings from the cloakrooms.
The best thing is to use a classroom and to place a desk across the
door so that no one enters except the attendants. If, in addition
the room is never left unattended, then this should be sufficient.
The usual system of cloakroom tickets can be worked with or
without a charge being made. In the case of the discotheques in
which I have been involved, I have usually set the entrance fee and
the cost of the cokes so high that when the cloakroom comes up
for discussion I lose my nerve and allow it to be used free of charge.

One of the things which strikes the teacher attending his first
discotheque is the sheer incredibility of the garments which many
of the girls turn up in. They give the appearance of having just
returned from rummaging about in the wardrobe department at
Sadler's Wells. It is enough to make even the most avant-garde
senior mistress shake her head and renew her determination to
resist the abolition of school uniforms.

Dress for Outings

To digress a little, the question of dress on out-of-school occasions
is important, especially with regard to older boys and girls who
may be growing weary of their school uniform. If the school has a
compulsory uniform then it is common to find that the head
requires the uniform to be worn on all trips out of school except
those which require special clothes — for scrambling up mountains
or along a coal face, for instance. This is often unpopular among
the boys and girls. The young ladies particularly resent being label-
led as sixteen-year-old school-girls when on an outing to London.
They would much prefer to come in mufti and live out fantasies
which involve looking at passing men from under hooded eyelids.

I once took a party to London on an occasion when the head, having been subjected to a little lobbying, had allowed the boys and girls, out of regard for their age and sense of responsibility, to wear their out-of-school clothes. The result was that they enjoyed the trip much more, but I did think that I was going to have to protect some of the girls from actual physical assault.

At the Newport Pagnell service station of all places, a coach bearing a lot of young men drew up alongside ours and a rather objectionable youth, volubly supported by his equally objection-able friends, sprang off and ran up to our coach beating the windows next to the girls, who did, I must say, look very presentable indeed — much too good for the likes of him. He was visibly water-ing at the mouth and giving vent to cries of "Get 'em off!" and other greetings of the kind which seem to be current these days among common clerks and apprentices.

It is my experience that whenever boys and girls are given the opportunity of wearing clothes of their own choice for an out-of-school function, they invariably turn up looking smart and fashionable. (Discotheques are exceptional — a sort of uniform is actually worn for them.)

The more one sees of this, the more difficult it becomes to sus-tain arguments in favour of compulsory school uniform. Those who support uniform, it is fair to say, would hold that for a special event, such as an outing, the boys and girls will make a special effort and that these standards would not be kept up day by day. I still have, though, a sneaking wish that more uniformed schools would take the plunge and give freedom a try.

11
Junior Schools

A lot of what I have written in this book applies to children of any age group. Special consideration for junior schools is by no means universally necessary. I am conscious, though, that my mind has been fixed fairly firmly upon a picture of out-of-school activities as they happen in a large secondary school. Junior school colleagues are becoming accustomed to this attitude, I think, and see themselves at times as a forgotten race. Certainly there are some secondary teachers who give the appearance of either refusing to acknowledge the existence of junior schools altogether — regarding them as figments of the fevered imaginations of people with names like Pestalozzi — or they seem to think of them as places where children are fed on scurrilous dogma involving coloured bricks and plastic jugs of water, instead of being taught genuine facts about capital cities and factorization.

To redress this balance a little, I propose to examine in this chapter some of the ways in which things are different in junior schools in the field of voluntary activities.

The thing which has struck me most forcibly about out-of-school activities in junior schools is that in one very important way the picture is an almost complete mirror image of what goes on in secondary schools. In a comprehensive school, for example, it is common to find that there are ten or a dozen activities in which any one child could join and that a number of these are only poorly supported — the choirmaster has to struggle to keep up his numbers, and the rugby team turns out with only thirteen men from time to time.

So the idea grows that in some secondary schools at any rate, there might almost be too great a variety of activities. The point is reached where to start another club or society is to take members away from existing ones.

In many junior schools on the other hand, the pattern seems to be that there are only a few activities and that these are heavily over-subscribed. I learned, for example, of a junior school — a fairly typical example — which had, apart from the ubiquitous football team of which more anon, only one group which met after school.

This was a P.E. club which had a long waiting-list of children who wanted to join, and an entrance test. Membership conferred upon the boys and girls a considerable amount of status among their fellows. The club was run by two or three men teachers who stayed behind once a week and supervised the children in what were fairly conventional gymnastic activities, with boys and girls leaping in all directions over vaulting horses, and swinging around like half-pint Tarzans.

The impression grows that in junior schools there are generally not enough out-of-school activities in the sense of clubs and societies meeting after school. Boys and girls of eight to eleven have not usually developed many interests in the world outside school, and they are singularly forthright in manner and lacking in the quasi-sophisticated indifference of attitude which will inevitably afflict them when they grow older. As a result, they will usually be willing to stay on after school for amost anything providing that it is moderately interesting and run by a teacher for whom they have some regard. There is a wonderful opportunity here to introduce young children not only to the hobbies and interests themselves, but also to the attitudes of mind which we associate with participation in voluntary activity.

This opportunity is, I feel, with many honourable exceptions, not always being taken to the full, I do not know why this should be. The cynical school-master will point to the large number of women teachers in junior schools and suggest that by five past four they are all hotfoot on the way home to get their husbands' tea ready. I hasten to say that I do not really see the truth of this when it is clear that other women, biologically and by qualification identical with their junior school colleagues, are to be found doing all sorts of after-school things in secondary schools.

A more plausible reason is that the organization of a junior school class demands that the teacher spends a fair amount in his or her classroom after the children have gone home, sorting things out and preparing for the next day. A junior school is also a smaller place as a rule, and even if a fair proportion of the staff stays behind, the total number will still be small, and there will

2B
MORRIS
DANCING

not be the large numbers of teachers milling about in the staff room and cooking meals that are likely to be found after hours in a secondary school. This latter atmosphere is self-generating. The more teachers stay behind, the more are likely to join them.

I need to say, I suppose, before I am speared to the floor by lady junior school teachers with blackboard compasses, that I am in no sense implying that nothing goes on in junior schools. It is simply that junior school children are so keen and interested that there is room for still more to happen. To any young teacher going into junior school work, I would say that he should do something with his children after school, no matter what, so long as it is legal and fairly safe. At that age, the children are very teacher-orientated, and staying after school with a teacher they like is more important than any consideration of what activity is actually going on.

One young junior school teacher — in his first year of teaching, in fact — decided to start a country dancing session after school. The fact that he knew as much about country dancing as a Mexican bandit knows about tossing the caber did not deter him in the least. He went to a few evening classes and learned some of the basic dances like Strip the Willow and some Morris Dances, including one which involved bashing sticks together in a manner likely to cause pain and bad language.

Thus armed, he went back and started his country dancing club. The kids loved it and turned up in droves. The boys particularly enjoyed the Morris dances, and bashed their sticks with such abandon that you could easily recognize them around the school by their blackened and swollen knuckles. The accompaniment was provided by the school record player, and the records were bought from the school's capitation allowance as P.E. equipment, which is not only legitimate but desirable.

Football

It is very apparent that the most important junior school out-of-school activity is association football. There are schools where the football team is the hinge pin of the whole establishment, its stars having the sort of cachet around the place which one normally associates with such worthies as George Best. This is in spite of quite a strong feeling in the world of P.E. and games that competitive inter-school football is not the thing for junior school children. Some towns do not have leagues or competitions for their junior school teams for this reason. In many cases, though, this policy is defeated by the teachers themselves, who arrange so many friendly games that an unofficial league competition develops.

The lengths to which some junior school colleagues will go to foster their football teams is rather disquieting. I heard of one school which actually brings its team back to school during the summer holiday for training sessions. The next development, I suppose, is to keep the boys incarcerated in school all Friday night, so that they do not have their strength sapped by over-indulgence in sherbet suckers and liquorice bootlaces. It is also common to find organized adulation of football teams being laid on in school assemblies. They are all called out to stand at the front, looking suitably modest as befits your young British sporting hero, while the rank and file who do nothing more worthwhile than play violins and write poetry, are allowed to clap until the headmaster raises his hand.

This is all a little distasteful. It encourages, I think, the sort of sporting hero cult to which we as teachers ought really to be try-ing to provide a counter balance.

The coverage of other sports is very patchy, and at least partly dependent upon the popularity of a given game in the school's home area and on the presence of knowledgeable and keen mem-bers of staff. Girls' games seem to be particularly poorly served in junior schools, though perhaps this is offset to some extent by the excellent dance activities which go on.

With younger children, the question arises as to how far teach-ers should allow themselves to go in their enthusiasm to introduce their own interests into school. There may well, at times, be too much of a tendency to push youngsters into things before they are ready. Junior school children are not just young adults, and those who teach them have to come to terms with childish attitudes and tastes.

Outdoor Activities

So, when I first heard of a junior school outdoor activities club, I felt that here was going to be an example of frustrated junior school teachers trying to pretend that their children are older and more mature in their tastes and abilities than they really are. In this I was wrong, and the venture which I was told about seems to have been well conceived.

The project was started by a group of teachers in an industrial town who wanted to introduce their children, at various junior schools, to some of the basics of outdoor life. They invited other

interested teachers to join them at a meeting and as a result an
association was formed which was really just a loose confederation
of interested schools.

A system developed whereby each school took it in turn to
arrange a day's walk on a Saturday or Sunday, and a group of
children and a teacher could come along from any or all of the
other interested schools. As a rule these walks were in the countryside just outside the home town and had the purpose, as well as
just giving the children an enjoyable outing, of introducing them
to the possibilities of their own home area as a place to walk about
in and enjoy. Occasionally they went further afield — to Derby-
shire and to the Malvern Hills, for instance — and on one or two
occasions there were overnight stays at youth hostels. Nothing too
ambitious was attempted though, and the children were never
pushed beyond the point of enjoyment and comfort.

As these rambles were made up of groups of children each with
their own teacher, the obvious point could be made that the schools
could easily have done this on their own. The fact is, though, that
up to that time they had not done so — the organization clearly
gave them the necessary push and was valuable for that reason.
Another point was that a new teacher, or one who was inexperienced in leading outings, was placed in a position where he could
take his own children out and yet still have the benefit of the
company and example of others more experienced. There was
obviously the potential here of a very useful piece of in-service
training for young teachers.

The whole thing was done with the approval and support of
the local education authority and the office of the P.E. organizer.
It would, indeed, hardly be possible or desirable to start such a
venture without this support. The authorities were able to ensure
that proper insurance cover was taken out for each trip and that
the rules regarding school outings were adhered to.

There were always more children wanting to go on these trips
than there were places for. The novelty of actually footing it
through the countryside on a summer Sunday, instead of sitting
in the back of a car in a traffic jam on the A5, clearly had many
attractions. The mums and dads were wildly enthusiastic too
for keeping the kids out of the way, it was considerably better

than Sunday School. I look forward to the day my own two girls can join such a venture.

The trips ran across one difficulty which is worth noting in case someone else starts up a similar scheme. In mixing together the children and staff of different schools, it was easy for a teacher to lose sight of his own children in the general mass. There was thus not the quick visual check on the presence and safety of the whole party which is available to a teacher who knows his own young-sters well by sight. It quickly became clear that however desirable it might be from the social point of view to have the children mingling together, there would have to be sufficient compromise to enable each teacher to be in effective charge of his own small group.

Co-operation

Co-operation between schools is seen a great deal in the junior field and is one of the attractive aspects of junior school out-of-school activities. Presumably it has something to do with the fact that the schools are smaller and physically closer together than are secon-dary schools, the two things combining to make working together both desirable and possible. Thus there are music festivals, drama festivals and folk dance gatherings which involve perhaps all the junior schools in a town or an area, and for which each school has prepared individually. The competitive element is usually left out of these festivals, as perhaps it should be, the emphasis being upon sharing and enjoying each others' work, and on combining in large-scale set pieces.

The important thing to remember about junior school activities is that they should be chosen with the ages and tastes of the child-ren clearly in mind. At secondary level it is easier to be convinced that adult type activities — or at least adult attitudes — are desir-able, for secondary schools do prepare children for adult life. It is the breakdown of this principle which leads to the worst aspects of junior school football, and the adherence to it which leads to the colourful inter-school drama and music festivals.

12

The Tuck Shop

The schools we used to read about, those strange places where chaps lived in dorms and shouted "cave!" at the approach of beaks, always had a tuck shop. It was, apparently, a real shop with an old besom behind the counter and rows of sticky buns on the shelves.

Far cry though it may be from the cloistered courts of Greyfriars to the bike sheds of an urban sec. mod., one thing which they are still likely to have in common is a tuck shop. In today's school, though, it will not be a warm little haven by the school gate, but a very ad hoc affair run by a teacher with the aid of a few cardboard boxes and a trestle table. He will in all probability be turning himself into a part-time confectionery salesman in order to boost the funds of his pet out-of-school activity.

If there is no tuck shop in a school, then it might be worthwhile for a money-seeking teacher to consider starting one. It is not the sort of thing to embark upon lightly, though for the difficulties are formidable

The usual thing is to procure supplies of what can best be described as child-centred footstuffs, and sell them from some strategic location during break.

What sort of money is there to be made? This varies considerably and depends on the size of the school and the affluence of the pupils. As an example, though, one school of twelve hundred pupils has two tuck shops, one each for the upper and lower school buildings. They are open only during the morning break — less than fifteen minutes a day. During this time they take between them, on a good day, about £8. About £2 of this ought to be clear profit. This, I repeat, is from two shops with two teachers.

One shop serving the same school population could not, in all probability, handle the same number of customers. As a rough guide, it is probably true to say that one teacher working with a group of pupil helpers can produce between £1—£2 profit a day. And £7 or £8 a week to spend on band instruments or sports equipment might seem considerably better than a kick in the teeth.

It is not so long ago, after all, that respectable members of the middle-class were expected to bring up law-abiding families on this sort of money.

The Difficulties

Before being seduced by the lure of untold wealth, however, let the prospective tuck shop proprietor be aware of the difficulties. For a start, there is the loss of the teacher's precious break time. Fifteen minutes in the staff room does not seem very much, but to have to work through this period — at speed and under pressure — for day after day is likely to cause the most energetic colleague to have second thoughts. It must, moreover, be every break. It might be possible very occasionally to ask a colleague to stand in for a session, but in fairness to the customers and to the children who are helping to run the shop, the normal routine must be for the master in charge to be present all the time. If he allows his supervision to slide through pressure of work or other commitments, or simply because he fancies a cup of coffee and a chat, then nefarious practices on the part of the pupil assistants are very likely to creep in.

If boys and girls are put in a position where they are surrounded by goodies and money then it is naïve to suppose that they will never take advantage of it, and unfair to continue to put them in the position of being so exposed. It will start in a small way at first — a biscuit each perhaps, or looking after friends in the queue by handing over free gifts. If it is not instantly made obvious that the slightest discrepancy can be detected almost immediately by the master in charge, then escalation of a galloping nature will rapidly set in. It is worth noting that if it is not money which is being taken but goods, the pilfering will not be detectable in the daily takings. It may, in fact, be a week or more before it is realized that the stock is disappearing at a faster rate than is warranted by the income. If the teacher starts off with the assumption that his helpers are, come what may, going to be honest then the theft can reach alarming proportions before it is discovered.

I have gone on a bit about this dishonesty business because I have found numerous examples of teachers who have made the mistake of assuming that because children are good natured and indeed quite honest in their ordinary day-to-day school life, they will all continue to be so when temptation is thrust in their way. It is unfair and foolish to make this assumption, and some who have made it have been caused considerable regret and worry.

In the long run, the avoidance of dishonesty is a matter of the relationship between the master in charge and his helpers; it is also a contributory factor if the children who help in the shop have an interest in the way the money is spent — the football team helping to sell so that they will have money for kit, for example.

There is, though, the need for continuing practical security measures. The master in charge should be behind the counter all the time the shop is open, taking direct charge of what is going on and also watching for the hands which sometimes creep from between closely packed customers and rapidly withdraw again clutching biscuits. This last possibility should be avoided by arranging things so that the situation does not arise of hordes of ravening youngsters pressed hard up against a counter which contains the goods. If there is no other way of doing it, then the items to be sold should be kept behind the servers rather than in front of them.

It might be worth using some of the profits to build an actual shop. A good look round the school will sometimes reveal a suitable empty space which can be pressed into service with the aid of a little woodwork. Often, the three cornered sort of gap which is left under staircases will be suitable and a shop front can be built to fill the space and provide a door and a serving counter. A wild hour or two with some paint and brushes and the whole thing can look quite attractive.

A word of warning about lettering. As one school I have visited found out, the word "Tuck" can be altered with comparative ease into something much less socially acceptable. The assistants at the school in question arrived one break to find that they were now apparently the proprietors of an establishment devoted to the gratification of appetites quite different from their original intent. They are now working under a sign which simply says "The Shop", and I would advise any beginner in the field so to label his establishment right from the start.

What to Sell

What should a tuck shop sell? The usual thing is to stock various lines of sweet and savoury biscuits and crisps and things. Actual sweets and chocolates do not go so well and probably deteriorate more easily.

There are moral issues involved, of course. The health authorities do not like children to consume large quantities of sugar and starch, for it does neither their teeth nor their figures much good. You have only to look at some adolescent girls to see what they mean. In fact, of course, the compulsive eating which some children indulge in probably has deep-rooted psychological causes. I teach history to a small class which has in it a girl who occasionally produces a jam sandwich with cries of: "Please, sir, I'm sorry sir, but this is an emergency, honest!" Such is the real urgency in her voice when she says this that I cannot but doubt her sincerity. As a matter of fact, though, she is one of the thinnest girls in the class, and her teeth look fine to me.

We cannot avoid, however, the responsibility which we have in health education. Things have gone a long way since the only thing we did for children's bodily health was to give them a spoonful of cod liver oil and a canter round the playground on a frosty morning. This being so, it probably says little for our integrity as educationists if we ourselves actually sell the children stuff which rots their teeth and inflates their bodies to the point of shapelessness.

But alas, the lure of profit is strong, and there is a tendency for these considerations of health to be conveniently forgotten. Various rationalizations are put forward of the kind used by those who seek to justify the selling of arms to South Africa, "If they did not buy them here they would buy them somewhere else."

The teacher who is going to start a tuck shop must make up his own mind about this. It is sometimes possible to make some compromise gesture. There may, for instance, be a limit on the amount which each child is allowed to spend. Indeed, if there is no such limit, then the teacher might have to step in and control things on an ad hoc basis from time to time, because there are always one or two children who have apparently unlimited

amounts of money and will happily stand at the head of the queue buying food in such gargantuan quantities and bizarre combinations as to make a squeamish adult feel quite faint with nausea.

Crisps and other savoury products are probably less objectionable on health grounds than are sticky sweet biscuits, and they are always popular. Crisps come in a large variety of flavours, and schoolboys rapidly become connoisseurs. Some schools, I am told, come to terms with the health thing by selling apples and nuts and other trendy fare. The takings in shops where they do this are never high, and the perishability of some of the items must make things very difficult.

Supplies of conventional tuck shop stock are never difficult to obtain. Any school is visited quite often by representatives of wholesalers, and it is simply a matter of coming to an agreement with one of them. The local man with his own van may prove to be more flexible to deal with than a rep. from a large concern. The smaller operator may well be able to pop some more stuff round if you run out during the week, and it might be possible to haggle with him over some of the discounts which he offers.

The stock needs to be carefully looked after. Bulk supplies should be kept under lock and key, preferably away from the tuck shop area itself, and one way of avoiding dishonesty is to count out from the bulk stock each day a given moneys-worth of goods and to point out to the sellers that at the end of the day's operations there should be stock and money which together come to the same value as the original amount. In this way there can be a running check on the stock.

Breakages can eat into profits quite considerably if the stock is not carefully handled. If a box of biscuits is thrown about or even dropped, a large proportion of its contents can easily be converted into biscuit dust, which is interesting stuff, but quite unsaleable. Those little dome-shaped chocolate covered marshmallow biscuits are popular and sell very cheaply, but they are fragile, and so packed that a ham-fisted lad will crush a dozen while trying to extract one from the box. When I had a tuck shop, we used to sell these marshmallows for one old penny each and it was not un- known for second-formers to come up with a bob, buy twelve and consume the lot at the rate of about three a second.

Litter is always a problem in schools. It may be controlled, so that the school appears tidy, or uncontrolled, in which case it will look like a tip. But in either case the problem is there, and a tuck shop does nothing to help. If care is not taken, the area where the customers congregate can become a squalid morass of discarded crisp bags and biscuit wrappers. It might be necessary from time to time to threaten to close the shop for a week or so, and to carry out the threat if necessary. At one school, there was sufficient space in the area round the tuck shop for benches and tables to be installed, providing an incentive for the children to stay and eat their bits and pieces in the one place. The surroundings were made quite attractive by means of painted decoration by the art teacher, and all the woodwork was done by the deputy head. Obviously it is no use sitting and waiting for the local authority to provide facilities of this sort. Schools which want more than the basics have to be prepared to pull themselves up by their bootstraps a bit.

This particular school has a coin-in-the-slot hot drinks machine installed in the tuck area, and a word about these will not come amiss. Salesmen from the firms which install these often visit schools and not unnaturally tell of the advantages and profits which will be forthcoming. Experience shows, though, that although such a machine is a useful facility, appreciated by the boys and girls, it might be unrealistic to look upon it solely as a money-making venture. When making the decision to install one, it would be best to consider its advantages as a service to the school community and to place thoughts of profit firmly in the background, because it is not often that a school hot drinks machine does very much more than hold its own financially. Seen even in these terms, though, they are useful to have around. A modern machine from a reputable supplier will prove reasonably reliable and the drinks which come out are more acceptable in flavour these days than they used to be.

The machine in the school to which I referred acts as a focal point where pupils gather at break and lunchtime and sometimes, illegally, for a quick moment of respite between lessons. Members of staff sometimes join them; we have, I suppose, discovered a modern equivalent of the fireplace or the stove which provided a "social point of focus" in older school buildings, a facility which is lacking in so many modern establishments.

Administration

In addition to the work of supervising a tuck shop, the teacher in charge will find himself involved in a fair amount of administration and book-keeping. The accounts have to be properly kept, and are subject to the inspection of the local authority's auditors, who visit schools at regular intervals. (They have usually dealt with school-teachers for so long that they are no longer surprised by the originality of their book-keeping methods, but it is best not to push their patience too far.)

One solution to the accounting problem is to allow the books to be kept as a practical exercise by pupils taking commercial studies, the master in charge of the tuck shop passing over to them his vouchers, receipts and other pieces of paper.

A bank account will also be necessary, both in order to simplify the accounting and to ensure that large amounts of money are not kept on the premises. There will have to be a weekly trip to the bank, which again means expenditure of valuable time.

Educational Benefits

I have hardly touched on the educational value of a tuck shop to the boys and girls who help to run it, but clearly this is one of the benefits to be gained. It is not simply a matter of using children as unpaid slaves and watching them like hawks to see that their pockets are not bulging with ill-gotten Jammie Dodgers or pound notes.

Less able youngsters are perfectly capable of handling the work in a tuck shop, and it is very common to find the remedial department closely associated with this sort of venture. Boys and girls from lower streams do not figure largely in orchestras and choirs; there are exceptions of course, but it is one of those nasty things in life that we have to face, that dull children are at a disadvantage in almost everything they undertake, not just in Maths and English. They do, however, like the sort of involvement which a tuck shop offers, and are less likely than more able children to become bored with the prospect of giving up every break time to the task of serving out endless crisps and biscuits. On the contrary, they usually enjoy the status and privilege this gives them.

The master in charge should inflate this feeling of importance as much as possible, by having them conduct as much of the business themselves as possible. They can go and see the head on matters of policy, receive supplies from the "biscuit man", accompany their teacher to the bank — worth more than any number of lessons on the subject in a Newsom type course — and ceremonially hand over things which have been purchased with the profits.

Boys who operated the tuck shop in one school used some of the money they made to buy good quality materials with which they made, helped by the metalwork teacher, a very attractive wood and metal reading desk as a feature for the main assembly hall. It stands there now as a continuing reminder that boys whose academic achievements are perhaps small, and who may be regarded by some as vagabonds and hooligans, are capable of making a tangible and worthwhile contribution to society.

13
Running a School Bus

Probably the most usual way of providing transport for school journeys is by hiring a coach, and in normal circumstances this will be the most convenient and reasonable in cost.

A lot of schools, however, feel that they would like some transport of their own, and quite a number have achieved this ambition. It is becoming increasingly common to see smart little buses running about, with the names of schools painted on the side, driven by track-suited P.E. mistresses; a big inter-school sporting fixture will produce a whole swarm of them.

The advantages are perhaps too obvious to require much detailing. The majority of teachers could find occasions in their work when the possession of such a vehicle would make their job easier. But it should also be remembered that owning a vehicle actually *creates* journeys. It is necessary to bear this in mind, because it might appear to a school which does not have one that the uses to which a bus could be put are too limited to make it worth-while. What is actually likely to happen is that all sorts of projects become possible which no one would have seriously considered before.

The type of vehicle to be bought depends largely upon the resources of the school. Obviously, the larger and more affluent the school the better the vehicle is likely to be. There is some obvious and seemingly unavoidable injustice in this state of affairs. Clearly the schools which really do need some transport of their own are the impoverished ones in deprived urban areas. A school which is surrounded by brick and concrete and peopled by children who badly need social and spiritual enrichment has a crying need for the partial liberation which a vehicle of its own could give. The schools which actually have the buses and coaches though, tend to be the ones which are already well supplied with the good things of educational life. The inequitable nature of the world is punched home even further in this context by the fact that it is the well-equipped large school which is in a better position to keep down its costs by buying a cheap vehicle and doing its own maintenance and conversion. By contrast a small school, or an older one with few workshop facilities or specialist staff, or a junior school with none of these things, will need to spend good money on a vehicle which will run reliably with little more than routine garage maintenance.

Unto the schools which hath it tends to be given, and a great shame it is too. One of the things which could be done to improve the lot of those schools which are not fortunately situated is to give them the where-withal to enrich their children's lives, and the authorities and the Government do try in some areas. A further real cause of inequity, and one which it is difficult to see any way out of, is caused by the fact that the glass suburban palaces are more likely to receive the help of the affluent parents of their children than are the Victorian brick inner ring schools. In the latter cases, the goodwill may be there in great abundance, and I know that many heads prefer this to the big hats and cheque books, but the practical difficulties are still there.

In at least one urban school I know of, for example, the usual process is reversed, and instead of receiving the largesse of a parent committee, the headmistress spends a lot of her time raising money to help the parents. It must be very frustrating to such a head to read of the town's direct grant grammar school being presented with a new minibus, something which as far as she is concerned is an impossible dream.

Converting a Van

As an example of what can be done relatively cheaply by a school equipped for the job, one school has had over the past ten years a succession of vehicles which has each cost under £50 to buy. Two or three of these were ambulances which had been pensioned off by the local council. Ambulances are, of course, beautifully maintained during their working lives — necessarily so if they are going

to start on the button when the phone rings and arrive safely with
their patients without the embarrassment of fetching out the RAC
when half way to hospital with a maternity case. When they are
eventually sold off, although they may well have a very hefty
mileage behind them, they are capable of giving good and reliable
service for a year or two if they are carefully looked after.

The school in question bought its ambulances for £40—£50 a
go, installed seats and put on a new coat of paint — although there
was always an exciting week or so during which the vehicle was
motored about in its original livery complete with red crosses.
Busy junctions presented no problem at all in these circumstances.

Only one ambulance was in any way a disappointment considering the low prices that were paid. It had some sort of weakness in
the chassis which was not obvious on visual inspection and which
only showed up on the road when enough confidence was gained
to drive at fair speeds. The frame tended to flex on corners,
making steering a somewhat hit and miss affair (and I use that
phrase advisedly). The technique for successful negotiation of a
sharp corner was to put on about three turns of steering lock
and then rapidly unwind most of it as the body rolled and chassis
attempted to tie itself in a knot. If you were a bit slow with your
reactions, you mounted the pavement on the inside of the bend,
to the consternation of unwary pedestrians. This disease is, I
believe, known in string-back glove circles as "roll oversteer".
The deputy head of the school, who drove the vehicle more than
anyone else — in fact, there were few who would go near it at all —
still holds the opinion that it was the only rigid vehicle in the
world with the capability of jack-knifing.

Needless to say, it was soon disposed of. A joke is a joke, and
indeed a drive in the errant ambulance was likely to provide
enough drinking stories for a week. I was told of one hair-raising
ride along the A45 which would have provided the material for
several Jacques Tati films — but the safety of children was involved
after all.

The most successful vehicle which this school bought was a
bread van. It was a one ton Morris Commercial which had been
deemed unworthy of further service humping Mother's Pride
round the streets, and which was bought from a dealer known to

someone on the staff, for the sum of £15. This sum apparently covered the dealers costs, which raises all sorts of frightening

questions about the level of profit which someone like this might expect to make in a normal deal with the public.

The vehicle was brought to its new home and the specialist departments of the school went to work. The metalwork department cut window holes in the side of the van, and installed standard aluminium framed bus windows bought from a vehicle breaker. They also put in bus seats obtained from the same source, being particularly careful when anchoring them to the floor. This care is necessary because when fifth-form girls are subjected to the normal laws of physical motion, the strain which the more rounded of them can place upon the seat anchorages almost defies

imagination. Needless to say, bread vans are not necessarily constructed with a view to accommodating these forces. The provision
of extra framing under the floor to take the seat bolts might well
be necessary, depending upon how many seats are to be installed.

The rear delivery doors were removed and replaced by a plain
panel incorporating a full width opening window which did
service as an emergency exit. A few coats of paint and some
professional looking lettering by the art department completed
the external and superficial work.

While all this was being done, the engine, gearbox and back
axle were removed and subjected to a thorough overhaul as part
of the school's motor vehicle engineering course. Close attention
was also paid to the brakes and suspension.

The existence of this specialist motor vehicle course, run by a
teacher with appropriate motor vehicle engineering skill and
qualifications, and of accommodation and equipment to suit, is
obviously at the bottom of the success of this school's policy of
buying cheap vehicles and keeping them on the road. A school
without such facilities would very quickly run into trouble if it
tried the same thing. This is shown by the fact that the school in
question finds that quite literally hardly a week goes by without
some fairly major work being needed on its vehicle — when children are being transported around there can be no "making do" or
compromising with factors involving reliability and safety.

This school's motor vehicle engineering course tackles quite
ambitious repairs, but it should be mentioned that while some
of the work can be done in school time as part of the course, this
will not by any means be enough, and the teacher who is in charge
of the maintenance of a school vehicle must be prepared to spend
a great deal of his own time in creeping about underneath it, and
in rushing about the countryside in search of spare parts. The
teacher who offers to look after a school bus, particularly an
elderly one, must, therefore, go into the job with his eyes open.
He must keep on top of the work. There must be no chance of a
colleague putting his foot on the brake one morning and finding
nothing there.

Maintaining an older vehicle clearly takes up an enormous
amount of somebody's time and provides a headache for everyone

involved, and there are patently grounds for believing that to buy a cheap bus is to practise false economy. It would be better, the argument goes, to lay out more cash in the first place rather than have highly qualified men and women taking up large amounts of their valuable time working on and worrying about a vehicle which is always on the point of breaking down. No one can really quarrel with this point of view, of course, but every teacher will

recognize that this is yet another of those situations, so familiar in education, when teachers have to mess about with lash-up situations which are in the long-run economic nonsense, simply because the hard cash is just not available to remedy the situation.

Buying Something Newer

Expensive though it may be, the school which does not have specialist motor maintenance facilities would be well advised to buy a new or nearly new minibus. This will cost at least several hundred pounds, and it is very easy indeed to get into four figures. A purchase of this sort requires a major fund-raising effort, and it is obviously the sort of project to which a parent's association might turn its attentions.

Another minor reason for involving the parents is because of the increased chance of finding someone who has a contact with the motor trade and who might be able to assist in finding a good vehicle at the right price. In any event, second-hand vehicles should

not be bought without expert advice, and that means a qualified
engineer, not just someone who "knows a bit about cars". It is in
fact possible to know a lot about cars and still not be qualified to
pronounce upon the fitness of a vehicle which is going to cost
someone a lot of money. If there is any doubt at all, the RAC or
the AA will provide an engineer to do an inspection, and this
service is extremely thorough.

If there are no trade contacts through which a reasonable price
can be negotiated, then some hard bargaining must be done. A
worth-while discount should be expected from the advertised price
of any new or used vehicle when there is no trade-in deal involved,
and the buyers must shop around the reputable dealers in the
district until the best price is forthcoming. It might be worth
suggesting that a handing over ceremony be arranged, with attendant free publicity for the dealer, or it might even be possible to
work out a deal where the vehicle carries the dealer's name fairly
prominently. Certainly no stone of this nature should be left
unturned.

I have tended to assume that a small bus of twelve to fourteen
seat capacity will be used rather than a full-sized coach. Some schools
do go in for larger vehicles, with the attendant advantages in terms
of space for camping or for accommodating a full class of children
at a time. My own feeling, though, is that there are enough disadvantages to tip the balance away from having one. A new or
nearly new coach is, for one thing, going to be too expensive for
most schools to contemplate buying. This means that an older one
will have to be considered, with all the accompanying difficulties
of reliability and maintenance which I have considered already,
but this time magnified enormously both by the sheer size of the
vehicle and by the fact that it will almost certainly have a diesel
engine which requires very skilled specialist care if it is to give its
best. (Most modern minibuses also have a diesel engine option,
but before falling for the idea of cheaper fuel costs, the buyer
should investigate the maintenance and servicing prospects very
thoroughly. The initial cost is also higher.)

A coach will also be much more of a handful in city traffic, and
it will not be possible to park it with the same ease and freedom as
a minibus which can, to all intents and purposes, go anywhere a

car can go. I also boggle a little at the thought of a frail school-mistress (or a frail school-master for that matter) trying to change a wheel on a coach after a puncture.

It is probably advisable then to eschew thoughts of booming off all over the place in a forty-five seat AEC, and settle for a Ford Transit, Leyland or Bedford, or any other of the very many sturdy and practical little buses which are on the market.

Legal Problems

Caution must be exercised in financing the running of a school vehicle. At the time of writing there is some prospect of changes in the laws which govern their use, so I will not go into the matter very deeply. I will say though, that the position at the moment seems to be that if any charge at all is made on the passengers who use the bus, then it is brought within the ambit of the Public Service Vehicle regulations, which involve a very stringent set of rules about construction and use of the vehicles and about the qualification of the drivers.

Obviously, the legal aspects must be gone into in detail, with learned advice, *before* any vehicle is bought.

And when you have your bus, please use it. Take it to sports meetings and concerts. Pop off to museums and canal locks. Go round touting for stuff for the jumble sale. Generally, in fact, make it work hard for its living. If you do this, it will repay its investment and add another dimension to the educational facilities which you can offer the children.

And, appropriately mentioned at the end of the chapter, buy or make a large flat trailer for it. This will justify its cost in the end by saving wear and tear on the interior of the vehicle when the need arises to transport bonfire wood or second-hand gas cookers.

14

Getting Them Interested

Most schools with which I have come into contact have been proud of their out-of-school activities. Head teachers and their colleagues are always happy to reel off long lists of clubs and societies and to fling open door after door, displaying chess clubs, choirs, debates, and all the fun of the fair in progress in every nook and cranny of the building all through the lunch-hour and far into the night after school.

Some teachers, though, are less satisfied. They will point out that, impressive though the total number of activities may be, this is too often accomplished by the same lively and intelligent youngsters rushing from one rehearsal to another. I was musing on this during a school carol service the other evening.

As it went on I became aware of a charming young lady of about thirteen who, in the space of about ninety minutes, sang in two separate choirs, read one of the lessons, played second violin in the orchestra and treble recorder in the recorder group. She is probably an extreme case, but if we look round carefully at the activities in our schools we will find that very often this sort of thing is, to a greater or lesser degree, responsible for their variety and for the amount of support which they receive.

In my own choir, for example, I have an alto who cannot come to practice on Mondays because she is chairman of the debating society, two or three members who miss one day a week to attend orchestra, and any number who blow recorders. The leading soprano is always in the school play, so we say goodbye to her when the production is imminent, and so it goes on.

Quite clearly, the activities of these youngsters are absolutely admirable, and we are privileged to work with them — they dispel our gloom on wet Mondays and generally make it all worth-while.

Nevertheless, it is true that because so much is done by so few, there must exist in a lot of schools a vast lump of humanity which attends lessons, passes an exam here and there, and goes out into the world without ever having done anything above and beyond the call of duty.

The name of it all is apathy, of course, and schools are not alone in being beset by it. I have just read of a meeting which was called to organize the annual carnival in the town of Leamington Spa. The meeting was attended by eight people, of whom about half were from the council and the police. If apathy were not such a widespread disease, we would find ourselves with much better councillors, magistrates and politicians than the ones we have foisted on us because we are so unwilling to take the jobs on ourselves.

A young teacher's heart can be broken by apathy. He comes into a school fresh and full of ideas, sets up his club or society and knocks himself out for the boys and girls, only to find that after a while, when the novelty has worn off, they yawn and drift away. Every teacher knows the heart-breaking feeling of running very hard in an effort to stay in the same place, of hoping that "next year" there will be a better football team, a bigger choir, or more members in the stamp club.

To try to pin down the apathy rate a little more closely, it can be no exaggeration that in most schools just about everything in the way of out-of-school activities is done by fewer than fifty per cent of the children, and I feel that this might be a generous estimate in some cases.

There are two aspects to this of course. On the one hand, we could assume that we need to reach into the mass of children much more than we do, and spend a lot of our time worrying about how to do this. On the other hand, we could hold that the children who are already taking part in activities are the ones to bother about, and that others, having been free to choose, have rejected the opportunities presented to them. Out-of-school activities are, after all, supposed to be run for the enjoyment of the children rather than for the recreation and diversion of the staff.

As usual, there is truth in both points of view. But we cannot ignore the children who take no part in school outside of lessons, for the very reasons which I gave as justification for out-of-school activities right at the beginning of this book. At the basis of our position as *teachers* is the assumption of the right to know what is best for our children.

But some of the non-participants will already be finding a full life outside school, like the girl in my tutorial group who is an accomplished gymnast and does almost all her training and competition at the local athletic institute with her boy-friend.

Reaching the Others

Attracting many youngsters to out-of-school activities is no mean task. Part of the trouble is that activities are not usually started on the basis of what the customers want. They are dictated by the specialist skills and interests among the available staff. I do not think that this matters overmuch. The children we are trying to reach have become apathetic about everything, including those activities which they profess to like. The reasons for this lie deep in the field of educational sociology and, interesting though they are, are outside the realm of this book.

The most elementary thing to be remembered by any teacher who feels that there are pupils who would enjoy his activity if they would only come along, is that recruitment is best made by personal contact. Notices in assembly or on a board are sometimes useful for giving information, but they will have little force in persuading children to change their habits. Pupils must be talked to and their confidence gained patiently over a long period of time. The point is sometimes reached where one can say, perhaps to a girl who is a potential choir member, that if she will agree to give it a try, then you will never mention it again, even if she decides not to keep up her attendance.

Discussions in class will be useful too; even if they do not produce a new found enthusiasm, they may well be a means of illuminating the attitudes of those who are reluctant to join — the teacher may even find that they are right and that he will have to make some changes.

In a school with a wide ability range, for instance, it is very common for lower ability children to say that if they join something which is dominated by clever pupils — as so many activities are — they are made to feel unwanted. They may or may not be right in their assessment of the situation, but the teacher who knows of this feeling will want to do something to avoid his group having the apparance of an élitist organization.

Wasted Talent

There is also the problem of the children who are known to have a particular talent, but who do not use it to the full. Is it right to assume that they should do more, or are we wrong to

apply our own standards in every case? And if we do want more from them, how much pressure are we justified in applying?

I can give two examples of the sort of pupils who will give rise to this sort of self-questioning among teachers.

One is a girl who plays the flute. She has more than the usual amount of talent, but considerably less than the usual amount of energy. She does not practise enough and attends rehearsals on a very hit and miss basis. In short, you could say that she has a gift which is going to waste. Some would suggest that she is wasting a gift of God, and thereby committing a sin. I prefer to think of it as being a situation in which she is denying herself a great deal of future pleasure. To have such ability and yet not to realize it to the full is to fail to achieve complete satisfaction. She does not

seem to mind this at the moment — boy-friends are more important, not surprisingly. No doubt, though, she will become yet
another of those frustrated adults who go about saying "If only . . ."
We meet them all the time at parents' evenings.

The other example is a West Indian lad of about thirteen. He is
a good runner, but a lazy one. He will do anything to avoid being
picked for the cross-country team, even to the point of running
slowly in the trials, and when he is picked his attendance is
unreliable.

What does one do about such as these? Is it right to push them,
or should we let them make up their own minds?

I suppose we can take it for granted that those in charge of
them will have tried to find out what lies behind their reluctance.
Whether, for instance, there is hostility at home to the sort of
activity which the school wants them to join. This is by no means
uncommon. There are mums and dads who not only will stay away
instead of coming to hear their children sing or to see them act
and play football, but will actually grumble because their offspring
are doing these things. At so many school concerts, plays and
matches, the most striking thing is the dearth of parents who have
turned up to support it.

Still, having gone through the possible reasons for a child's
reluctance and eliminated the obvious ones, how far is it right to
push or even bully a child into taking part? Are we in fact right to
act on our own ideas and assume that we are right and they are
wrong?

There is no glib or universal answer, but I believe that we have
to make some sort of response to the problem. We cannot shirk
our responsibility. The very same questions arise in the classroom
situation, and in that context we have few qualms of conscience
about the correctness of applying a little pressure to our charges
in order to produce some results.

We should, in fact, be ready to press our reluctant ones a little —
to employ, if you like a little of the "You *will* enjoy yourself"
philosophy. The fluting young lady should be leaned on to give a
little more of herself in return for the time and energy, to say
nothing of money, which have been lavished on her. The boy
athlete should be made to turn out and run.

We owe this to the boys and girls themselves, and indeed to the others who are less talented but more keen. How frustrating it is for the "slogger" in a team to turn out patiently week after week and to feel that the teacher in charge is being taken for a ride by a clever individual who is being allowed to get away with murder because his abilities are too great to be dispensable.

Obviously there is a way of going about our pressurizing. It should be handled in a friendly way by a good-humoured and sympathetic teacher. Overt whip-cracking in the out-of-school field is too easily counter productive. There must be firmness, and to be firm and yet good-humoured with children who have perhaps not yet seen enough of life to appreciate to the full the nuances of personal relationships is a job which taxes the abilities of the best of us.

In the last analysis this is a matter of the relationship between teacher and pupil. If this is good, then the reluctant musician and the lazy runner will continue to turn out, albeit protesting the whole time.

Inducement

It is possible to use various ploys to increase the pressure. When I formed my choir at school, I sent individual letters of invitation to all those children and teachers whom I thought might be interested, and I still address them in this way quite often. I feel this is better, as I have already said, than impersonal notices on the board or read out at assembly. As far as choirs go, it should be a matter of music department policy that any pupil who is studying music for public examinations should be expected to sing in the school choir.

As far as increasing the discipline within a group goes, it is a good idea to encourage the members' sense of loyalty by allowing them to be, as far as possible, self-governing. Each out-of-school activity group should have its own committee, and the members should have a real say in policy-making.

If I can be forgiven for drawing yet another example from my choir, another device which I use to hold the loyalty of members and to ensure their support for particular functions is to write the date of each forthcoming engagement on a large sheet of paper and then have members sign up, a week or two beforehand, their intention to be there. The act of picking up a pen and writing one's name makes the commitment a little more real than simply raising a hand at rehearsal, or mumbling assent in company with everyone else.

Then there are all the usual carrots — the badges and prizes, rewards to which the faithful can aspire; there is nothing a young boy likes better than to be festooned with tin badges, and a good teacher will make the most of this. There ought to be several assemblies every year in which all the staff are bored utterly to tears for what seems like hours while endless streams of kids come up on the stage to have a handshake from the head and a badge pinned on them, or a certificate handed over for swimming, running, playing the sousaphone, or anything else that is capable of being thus rewarded — and I defy anyone to find an activity that cannot be so recognized.

Obviously I am a believer in the application of pressure. We really do know better than the children what is good for them. Make no mistake, if we do not believe this then we disbelieve in the need for professionally trained teachers at all, for anyone would be able to do the job. We must keep our humility, however. The knowledge of our superior wisdom should weigh us down with a feeling of responsibility rather than puff us up with a sense of our own importance, and under no circumstances should it cause us to close our minds to the thoughts and opinions of the youngsters.

15
Out-of-school Activities for Teachers

It is natural, I suppose, that in any school, and particularly in large ones with staff up to a hundred or so strong, that the teachers will develop a set of communal out-of-school activities of their own. These will range all through the spectrum from party visits to the theatre to end-of-term pub-crawls.

There are those who frown upon things like this and who mentally shrink away in horror if they find that they have joined a school which has an organized staff-room social life. To these reluctant ones, school is a place where one does a day's work and which ought to be left firmly behind in the evenings and at week-ends. The idea of mixing with one's colleagues outside working hours fills them with incipient hysteria.

You can see what they mean, and to some extent you can even sympathize with them. Teachers en masse are not a very prepossessing bunch — you only have to read the union conference reports to see that. There is among them a pronounced tendency to be at one and the same time dull, naïve, pompous and petty. It is also common to find a distressing tendency to carry into private life the minutiae of classroom routine. This was brought home to me on one occasion when I went to a party given by a friend and colleague in the next town. A lot of his fellow teachers were there and it was so depressing to observe them, sitting round on the floor looking like lower middle-class copies of a colour supplement advertisement, and talking all the time about their school and the horrible kids they were expected to teach. You know the sort of thing well, I expect:

"I had to take a house point from Greta Cattermole for

CHEWING again today. You should have seen the look she gave me."

All I can do, though, is to encourage new colleagues and those who are trapped among the pedagogic bourgeoisie that there are in fact a lot of teachers who can lay a fair claim to normality, and plenty of schools where the staff have a full social life together in sufficient variety to suit all but the most misanthropic tastes.

Staff Organization

In many schools the activities are organized by a properly constituted staff-room association with a committee and a sub-scription and all the other organizational paraphernalia. In spite of the appearance of bureaucratic proliferation which this tends to create, there are a lot of advantages in being properly organized, especially in a large school. For one thing, the regular events such as the staff Christmas dinner can be correctly run instead of being left to a few volunteers and the element of chance. In addition, day-to-day matters such as the provision of tea and coffee for flagging colleagues can be brought under proper control. More important than any of these though, is the fact that a staff-room association can act as a channel of communication between the headmaster and his staff.

An important side effect of the provision of a staff-room association is that the existence of a democratically elected staff committee tends to emphasize the all-important fact that outside their departments all teachers are equal; there are colleagues who are a bit rank-conscious at times, perhaps recalling happier days when they were adorned with pips and stripes and given their right-ful amount of deference. The staff-room association can remove a little of the wind from the sails of such as these, and serve perhaps to remind them that the holding of a scale five post does not carry with it the automatic right to appropriate the best locker or jump the coffee queue. By the same token the hierarchy of the school can divest themselves of their rank when they enter the staff-room. The head, indeed, will probably not find it appropriate to enter the staff-room very often, and the existence of a staff-room association will make it easier for him to stay away.

The actual activities which teachers share together outside school
vary greatly and all I can do is to indicate some of the ones which
have come to my attention. There are schools, for instance, which
have a staff evening at regular intervals, when the school facilities
are used for badminton or swimming, for art and drama. Activities
of this sort are very valuable for young members of staff living in
lodgings, and can do much to overcome the loneliness they might
otherwise experience in a strange town. Because of this, the young
teacher who takes as his first post an appointment in a large school
might well have something of an advantage over those of his
colleagues who go to small ones.

In a village school that I know of there is a young man on a
staff which consists, apart from him, entirely of a handful of
elderly men and women. No matter what good will there is, there
must be times in these surroundings when his difficulties seem to
be magnified out of proportion. If he were surrounded by people
of his own generation, things might appear very differently.

Staff Games

Large schools are often able to field staff teams in various sports
and games and can fill up a regular fixture list. Cricket seems to be
the most popular. The combination of warm weather, absence of
athleticism and the prominent part played in cricket by ancillary
equipment, such as the common beer pump and the pint mug, all
make it more attractive to the average middle-aged school-master
than other more muscular pursuits.

One staff cricket team of my acquaintance spent the whole
season in keen anticipation of a newly negotiated match against a
top class ladies XI. They half expected their opponents to be old
besoms of less than prepossessing appearance who would take
little part in the post-match carousing. Nothing could have been
further from the truth, and Sir Henry Newbolt would have been
proud to observe the way in which deathless friendships were
cemented both on and off the field of play that day, in the finest
public school tradition.

The boys and girls, in case we have forgotten them, take a very
keen interest as a rule in their staff's sporting activities. They

attend the matches in fair numbers partly, I think, out of sheer astonishment that their teachers are physically capable of such things, and partly in the hope of seeing someone maimed. Such is professional self-regard that the latter occurrence is fortunately

rare, but the spectators are often, as a compensation, made to realize that their heroes have feet of the finest kaolin.

This happened to a P.E. teacher I heard of. After spending years exhorting his teams on to acts of sportsmanship in the face of adversity — losing well, accepting decisions and so on — he was seen by a good gathering of his pupils to forget himself completely in a staff basketball match and knock a troublesome opponent unconscious with one swift and unerring blow to the chin. After that, of course, he could do no wrong in his pupil's eyes — there must be a moral there somewhere that would shock our Victorian ancestors.

Basketball is becoming almost as popular as cricket among the younger teachers. The facilities are usually present on school premises, and it usually finishes well before closing time. In my experience, though, inter-staff basketball games are remarkable for the amount of needle which creeps in — as the incident just recounted shows. And only the other night I sat next to a player, temporarily off court, watching a game between our staff team and another. My colleague kept breaking off conversation with

me to divert himself by clutching at the shorts of opponents as they ran past, apologizing profusely whenever he was detected. Perhaps, though, this particular chap should not be taken as a good example, as he kept referring to one of the other side as "their scrum half".

Staff Play

Sport apart, the highlight of the lives of many staff-rooms is the annual staff play. I am never sure about recommending to other staff-rooms the practice of putting on a staff play. There are obvious advantages in terms of morale and indeed of practical experience of dramatic work, from both of which the work of the teachers may benefit. They do however tend to take up an inordinate amount of time, and the situation can develop in which classes are receiving only cursory instruction because the energies of their teachers are being directed towards learning lines or painting scenery. I can also visualize a state of affairs in which morale does not improve but rather deteriorates, with people being offended left, right and centre, or finding new reasons for hating their colleagues.

Still, a staff play can be a lot of fun, and if it is carefully chosen to make the maximum use of the talents available, it ought not to place too much strain on the company. I always think that the best staff plays are those which have some music — enough to liven things up a bit, but not enough to complicate rehearsals too much.

Rehearsals are the bane of staff dramatic productions. Every one which I have experienced has entered the final week before the opening in a desperate state of unpreparedness. This is because the participants never show any sense of urgency whatever until about a fortnight before the opening night. At this point they wake up and begin to blame the producer for the fact that everything is behind schedule. What the producer must do at this point (an experienced one will, in fact, have waited in cold blood for this moment to arrive) is to publish a long list of rehearsals which are intended to take up every available lunch-hour and which go on from four-thirty to ten every evening, culminating in a grand all day session on the final Sunday, with the young ladies of the staff cooking hot dogs and heating up soup.

In all this, teachers show a remarkable reluctance to follow the precepts which they set before their pupils. They arrive late for rehearsals and miss them completely for the most trivial reasons. They argue with the producer, take the huff, talk instead of listening, and generally act like caricatures of all that their pupils are ever told not to be.

Such is the native wit and talent of most of the teachers I know, however, that against all the odds they seem to get away with it to the extent that the finished product is usually considerably more than adequate. Subterfuges creep in of course, of the kind advocated by Michael Green in "The Art of Coarse Acting" — things like writing lines on Roman spears and inside hats.

The children will flock to see any staff production. The sight
of their teachers falling about on the stage is more than they can
resist. Light-hearted stuff is probably best for teachers surfeited
with examination preparation and the pastoral care of wayward
kids.

A Working Staff Association

At this point I propose to give some details of one particular staff-
room association which I learned of in a comprehensive school.

It was an association which catered for a staff of about seventy
teachers. All of them were deemed by the rules of the association
to be members whether they liked it or not, and they had to pay
an annual subscription. This entitled them to use the staff-room
facilities and they could drink as much tea and coffee as they
wanted. There were times when the consumption reached such
proportions that the members were sure they were well in line for
a silver rosebowl or something from Maxwell House. Visiting
students on teaching practice were a heavy burden in this respect.
Their timetables were only partly filled, and in any case your
modern student drinks so much instant coffee that if he dropped
dead you could easily freeze-dry him and use him again without
anyone being wiser. At any rate, to make up for their constant
thirst, they were charged a subscription which was, pro-rata, considerably higher than that paid by the incumbent staff. The staff,
let it be said, also derived benefit in that it was hardly possible
for them to enter the staff-room without having a cup of coffee
thrust at them by some hairy chap.

The association's finance was handled by a treasurer who lived,
as all such people do, in a permanent state of anxiety about the
state of the accounts. This official also looked after the purchase
of drinking materials, buying them in bulk from a cash and carry
warehouse. There was also a secretary who looked after the correspondence but who resolutely refused to sit on the chairman's
knee, and a chairman who was generally supposed to hold a
position of prestige among his fellows. He had an intangible sort
of task which involved keeping his ear to the ground and generally being concerned about the well-being of the staff. As he was

elected by the staff, and was very much a rank and file teacher rather than a head of department, he was in a very strong position in many ways to know exactly what the feelings of his colleagues were. He could act as a channel between them and the head in that he was able to let the head know the staff's feelings on any particular point, and in return the head could make known his own opinions and feelings on those occasions when official communication via the hierarchy might have been inappropriate.

These officers were supported by a hard-working committee and once a year the whole bag of washing was subjected to re-election or rejection by the annual general meeting.

At the beginning of term, the committee and officers met to outline a programme of social events for the year. These normally comprised a fairly predictable succession of wine and cheese parties, musical evenings, literary evenings, dances and dinners. The musical evenings were something of a speciality with this particular staff, because there seemed to have gravitated to this school a fairly high proportion of musically talented individuals. The musical frolics were organized by the head of the music department, who always appeared three seconds before the starting time and began to write out a programme. Food was always served, and one teacher I spoke to has a painful recollection of taking a large bite off a lump of celery just as one of the performers was about to start a solo on the clavichord. I don't know if you've ever heard a clavichord, but if you have, you must have been pretty close to it at the time, for it is not an instrument for the hard of hearing. As a result, this music-lover was forced to sit for several minutes with watering eyes and bulging cheeks because of his natural well-bred reluctance to shatter the calm and magical atmosphere with loud donkey-like crunching noises.

One summer evening an art evening was held in the grounds of the country mansion where the art mistress had a flat. The staff and their friends painted and took rubbings — there was in fact a serious misunderstanding when someone asked the lady in question if he could nip down the garden and rub her gazebo. Later on there was a sort of action painting session involving the pouring about of boiling pitch. One of the young art teachers produced by this means a life-size rendering of a skeleton, which is now being used by the school's biology department to mislead pupils about the nature of the human body.

The success of all such occasions depended always upon the enormous goodwill of the lady members who did all the cooking and domestic arrangements. Functions which were advertised as wine and cheese evenings were, to my own knowledge, metamorphosed by these versatile folk into full scale nosh-ups, with the cheese hardly visible among all the other goodies.

The officers of this particular staff-room association were constantly being asked for advice by teachers in other schools who were trying to start something like it themselves, and this demonstrated, I think, that there is an increasing awareness of the need for staff-rooms to be organized. This is obviously a result of the growth in the size of schools, and the fact that in a large school many things have to be dealt with by proper decision-making and communication machinery which in a smaller establishment could be done informally without anyone feeling that there was any lack of consultation.

A newly formed large school — whether created from scratch or by amalgamation — has a particular need for some form of staff organization, and action on this should be taken very early in the school's existence before cliques and groupings have begun to form, and while there is still time for the voice of the teachers to be heard on the subject of the school's organization. Such an association can protect the interests of the staff in, for example, the provision and equipment of the staff accommodation.

No head that I know of resents or opposes the existence of a staff-room association — indeed, such is the power of most heads that no such organization could exist without his approval. In fact, the existence of an association can be advantageous to him in many ways. Through the chairman he has contact with the staff-room, and because so many aspects of routine staff-room life are being run the committee, he and his deputy are freed from some of the minutiae of administration which would otherwise have to be done, or at least overseen, by them.

It is my serious advice, for what it is worth, that any staff-room with more than about twenty-five members which is without a staff-room association should take steps to start one forthwith.

The advantages which accrue in terms of ease of communication, feeling of community and growth of efficiency in the day-to-day life of the staff-room, and the consequent increase in the morale of the staff, are far too great to be passed off. There is hard work in store for someone, though, and it might be best to ensure that the most onerous offices are filled by teachers who do not have heavy departmental responsibility. There are obvious diplomatic reasons, too, why this latter point should be desirable.

16
Parent Teacher Associations

Even though children are often not directly involved in their activities to any significant degree, parent teacher associations can usefully come within the terms of reference of this book. Enough out-of-school time is certainly spent by some colleagues on parent teacher committees to justify their inclusion.

Not every school has a P.T.A. and this is due in at least a proportion of cases to the reluctance of the head concerned. Only recently I read a letter in a Sunday paper from a bewildered father, in which he detailed his efforts to form a P.T.A. for the school which his sons attended. He was, it seems, frustrated at every turn by insurmountable difficulties which the headmaster of the school was, lo and behold, constantly discovering. Direct approaches to the managers bore no fruit either because they would go no further than to pass on his thoughts to the head.

It was clear to any teacher who read this letter that there was here a clear-cut case of a head who had absolutely no intention of allowing a P.T.A. to be formed at that particular moment, and was being a little circumlocutory in his methods. A direct and point blank refusal might have been more honest if less tactful.

The letter was, in fact, followed up by one from a head who pointed out that this was what was obviously happening. He added for good measure, that he believed that parent to be "arrogant" for daring to want such a thing, because they were unnecessary. The approach to the governors he clearly considered to be a crime only slightly less heinous than high treason. This letter in its turn, raised the hackles of a lot of liberal spirits, but the only remarkable thing about it was that it contained a lot of things which many heads feel but prefer to leave unsaid for fear of starting unnecessary argument.

The reasons for this fairly common unwillingness to start a
P.T.A. are varied. Some heads are undoubtedly motivated by feelings of insecurity. There is a reluctance to expose any part of their
school's activity to the probing gaze of the parents of the children
involved. Others have a more understandable and in many cases
quite justified fear that there will be, in one guise or another,

attempts at interference in those internal affairs of the school
which are properly and legally the concern of the head and his
staff.

Quite obviously this sort of thing happens rarely, but there are
heads who will not start a P.T.A. because they know some of the
parents who are waiting to join, and estimate that there is more
than the usual chance of unpleasantness arising. I know of more
than one head who has deliberately deferred the formation of a
P.T.A. until a particular child with an "awkward" parent has left

the school.

If a neighbourhood contains a group of people known to be opposed to the ideals of a school, you can hardly blame a head who wants to deny them a captive audience on his own premises.

The point is that our schools are organized in a way that places responsibility for what goes on in them firmly upon head teachers. There is no direct way by which any of this responsibility can be passed to the parents, and as a result a dissenting P.T.A. will achieve little other than factious argument.

Perhaps in time to come the boundaries around our schools will relax, but in the meantime democracy in terms of parental participation in decision making has a very long way to go.

Thus, no P.T.A. can exist without the consent of the head, and this consent is unlikely to be forthcoming unless there is reasonable certainty that the committee (for it is the committee which matters; large-scale apathy affects parents as much as it does teachers and pupils) will be, if not a bunch of yes men, at least in possession of views which are in accord with the overall policy of the school as laid down by the head.

The major aim of any P.T.A. is to add the time and talents of the parents to the general effort of running a school in those areas where such help is appropriate. The most common way in which this is done is by fund-raising. It may not often be stated that the be all and end all of a P.T.A. is to raise money for its school, but this is certainly what it all boils down to in very many instances. It seems as if almost every school which one enters can boast of a piano, a set of curtains, a panelled hall, or almost anything you care to name, which have been provided "by the parents". Pick up an evening paper and there is a good chance that you will see, on almost any day of the week, some parental chairman being flung into a newly opened pool with his clothes on.

I am never sure how defensive one ought to be about regarding the major function of such an association as being that of helping the school to buy things. The Liberal which stirs dimly within me says that I ought to welcome the idea of having parents dodging about in schools making themselves generally useful, and then meeting in the evening to decide whether the staff are behaving themselves.

There is nothing wrong with having them in school doing bits and pieces, of course, and this sort of thing is done in a lot of places. The union attitudes tend to be a little sensitive and short-sighted, but it is not too difficult to ignore them. After all if we took too much notice of our unions we would never give extra lessons during the lunch-hour or after school.

The limiting factor in having parents in school is not what the unions say; it lies in the matter of legal responsibility. This rests

only with the head and his staff. How far it is fair to have parents in school when they cannot really progress beyond doing odd jobs here and there or perhaps listening to children learning to read, when it is not possible in return to give them a voice in the formation of policy, is a moot point.

As to the matter of parents meeting to decide on curriculum policy and the suitability of teachers and their methods, perhaps it may come, but not, I hope, before I retire in about thirty years' time. I feel myself to be under quite enough pressure already, what with a head, a deputy head, a senior mistress, inspectors and numerous heads of departments all breathing down my neck. The feeling that I had to justify my actions to the parents of my children in anything other than the usual informal way at a parents' evening over a cup of tea would be more than I could bear. In those parts of the U.S.A. where P.T.A.s are powerful, some remarkable and indeed tragic things have happened, and it would seem that to democratize education by putting power in the hands of the community of parents is by no means a guarantee that democratic policies will be pursued.

In general, of course, teachers have a defensive attitude towards their professionalism. They see themselves threatened by amateur decision makers on local councils and P.T.A. committees.

Not that you can altogether blame them. Teaching is the job above all others that everybody thinks he can do, and the amount of free advice which we receive in pubs, on holiday and in the correspondence columns of the local press would fill several rather bizarre textbooks. The result is a tendency for the profession to scream loudly at anyone who claims to know more about kids than teachers do — even if the would-be usurpers of the teacher's role are the parents themselves.

Setting up an Association

The P.T.A. about which I have learned most is not in fact called by this title at all. It was decided at its foundation that there may be people other than parents and teachers who wished to join, and in fact a number eventually did so. The school groundsman, for instance, and the local doctor both found themselves elected to the committee. Because of this broadening of the membership beyond parents, it was decided that the organization should be called the "Friends of the School".

This particular group of "Friends" was formed out of informal contacts between the head and a number of interested parents. It came into being officially after a letter was sent to all the parents of children in the school, and to others who might be interested, asking them if they would care to attend a meeting in the school hall to discuss the project.

A hundred or so parents attended. This figure represents a very small proportion — in fact about one-twentieth — of the potential

number who might have come. Most P.T.A.s in fact are representative of only a small number of parents, and because the ones who
are interested are likely to be the more articulate ones, probably of
middle-class or professional background, a lot of these organizations are open to the charge of being rather narrowly based. Exactly
what can be done about this is difficult to see. Working-class mums
and dads are not, on the whole, participants and talkers, though
there are certainly exceptions, and although every effort might be
made to bring them in, it remains true that with the best will in
the world the image of the average P.T.A. is a middle-class one.

At this "Friends" meeting, a committee was elected which was
charged with the task of bringing the organization into active being.
The head avoided being elected chairman, and the post went to
one of the parents. It is, I feel, important that this should be so.
Control of a meeting which consists largely of parents comes best
from another parent. In this way the possibility of any muttering
about the school controlling the goings-on is avoided.

Besides the chairman, the committee consisted of a fair cross-
section of parents, two or three members of staff and two members of the pupil body of the school. This was a secondary school,
and the pupil committee members were both from the sixth-form.
Quite aside from the valuable contribution which they were able
to make as committee members, their presence on the committee
was a useful ploy for gaining the support of the older pupils for
whatever functions were likely to be planned.

There was a great deal of talk about the aims of the organization, but the major activity has been, inevitably, the raising of
money. The members seem to enjoy this very much. Many of them
have some spare time and energy and there is the feeling that at
last they are able to get stuck in and do something which will
benefit "their" school.

Of course, a great deal of benefit is to be gained in the form of
side effects from the actual money-raising activity. The parents
are brought into the school for their meetings, and in planning
and running functions children, teachers and parents are brought
together on ground where none of the three groups is likely to
have much advantage over the others. This can only be to the good.

A teacher sees a child in a different light if he spent the previous evening helping him and his mother to sell jumble or to label bottles for a stall.

In the association under consideration, the most successful functions from the point of view of mixing have been the dances held in the school hall. Parents reluctant to attend meetings come to these so there is a closer approach to a true representation of the school's parents. To see pupils, parents and teachers shaking a nifty leg together on the dance floor is to begin to believe in the ideals of the parent teacher movement.

The Teacher's Role

One of the difficulties which faces some P.T.A.s is the conversion into reality of the "T" part of the title. Teachers are naturally shy of such organizations, and it is often difficult for those who are duty-bound to support them to convince their colleagues of the importance of a show of enthusiasm from the staff-room.

Thus, a teacher who sits on a P.T.A. committee will find himself in difficulty from two directions. On the one hand he will have to persuade often reluctant or sceptical colleagues to give some support, and on the other he will have to watch with a careful eye the proceedings of the committee, some of whose members will assume that the staff of the school are waiting around twiddling their thumbs and dying to be relieved of their boredom by the privilege of making and doing things for the P.T.A.

In the end, staff are best won round by demonstrations of the practical value of the P.T.A. in terms of actual hard jingling cash for teachers to use in pursuit of their pet educational obsessions. The teacher representative must become hardened to the practice of going up to colleagues and saying such things as: "You will be pleased to hear that the P.T.A. voted £12 for a camping stove last night. I trust we will see you behind a stall at the summer fair?"

The problem of protecting one's colleagues from the demands of the committee is one which requires a greater degree of delicacy. Parent committee members are apt to believe that because they are raising some money, and because there is a staff of anything up to a hundred highly qualified folk about the place, this gives them unlimited scope for getting posters made, amplifying equipment set up, teas made and so on. It is also easier to call on the staff because they are on the spot with their equipment, and with large amounts of free sweated labour in the form of the everloving kids.

This all sounds so natural and reasonable to many, that they become offended when reluctance is shown. It might be necessary to point out that education must go on, and that even though their own demands may have educative qualities, it may be difficult to fit them in with the ideas of the teachers in question, to say nothing of the external examination syllabus.

The only answer to all this is good committee work. A teacher who has a talent for this sort of thing has a lot to offer to a P.T.A. committee, and it is true that successful and meritorious service on the P.T.A. committee never did anyone's career prospects any harm. It may happen that a young teacher is asked to do this sort of service because others are reluctant. The thing to do is to turn it to advantage and settle down to being noted for hard work, diplomacy and tact. It may well pay dividends.

17
Some Legal Pitfalls

I am a great believer in the principle of taking specialist advice
from specialist sources. For this reason I am most reluctant to
pontificate about the legal aspects of out-of-school activities. In
no sense am I legally qualified, either by learning or by conviction
(I couldn't resist that!) and I can make little claim to special knowledge or offer any guarantee of accuracy. The proper action for a
teacher who requires legal advice is to go to the legal department
of his union or professional association, or to make enquiry of the
officers of his local education authority.

What I can do is to point out those areas where the law impinges
upon the responsibilities of a teacher, with special regard to out-
of-school activities, and as it were to jangle the odd warning bell
so that he will be able to take the necessary steps to find out more
about the legal position. This is necessary because we are all very
apt to do things without ever taking into account the legal implications. A teacher can quite innocently, for instance, by such a
seemingly innocuous action as the preparation and production of
a play, involve himself in the breaking of all sorts of laws, some of
which he probably never even knew existed.

After-school Supervision

To begin with, let us consider the position of the teacher who
stays behind with his children to supervise them in an after-school
activity. It is important to realize that his responsibility of care to
them is not lessened at all by the fact that school hours have finished.
Neither is importance placed upon the fact that the activity is
voluntary both for him and for the children. His responsibility is
the same as it is during the working day. Therefore the rules under

which his club operates must take full account of this, and extra
freedom for the children, or a more informal atmosphere, must
not imply any decreased vigilance on his part. If games are
involved, the accepted laws or rules must be kept to, because it is
as well, if any harm comes to a child, to be able to show that the
normal procedures were being followed.

School Trips

Obviously, the duty of care extends into out-of-school trips and
outings, and continues for as long as the children are in the care
of the teacher. The time-honoured custom which many children
observe, of shouting from the back of the coach: "It's ten past
four, sir you can't touch us now!" has in fact no basis in law.

Regrettably, some teachers are deplorably lax about school outings, either through ignorance of the right thing to do, or because
of the old story of familiarity breeding contempt. For a start,
there is the matter of parental permission. It may or may not be
legally necessary for written permission to be obtained from the
parents of every child who is going on a school trip, but the point
should at least be considered and investigated, and not simply left
to go by default as it so often is. It is very easy to send out a duplicated slip, incorporating the granting of permission, and providing
for the indemnifying of the school against claims, to be signed and
returned. Whatever the legal force of such a document, it can do
no harm, and would at least provide evidence of some care and
concern if any trouble arose.

Supervision on an outing should be close and continuous unless
some special arrangements have been made for some unsupervised
activity to take place — as I described in the account of the trip
to London in Chapter Six. The danger is that teachers who are
friends will group together and give their attention to each other
rather than to their charges. This sort of thing can easily happen,
for instance, during a meal break. Theatre trips are often a source
of annoyance in this respect too. It is very vexing for a teacher
who is looking after his party carefully and at great inconvenience,
to find that they and he are being disturbed by children from
another school who are being supervised, or rather unsupervised,

by a group of teachers who are cosily gathered round a box of
Black Magic. Any teacher who is subjected to this should seek out
the offending colleague and at least point out that there is some
inconvenience being caused. In this way he will have a good jump-
ing-off point if there is trouble over an incident involving his own
children together with the offending ones.

Some children can render almost any activity dangerous. Leave
a knitting class alone for ten seconds and you might return to find
a child walking about the room with a number four needle sticking
out of the top of her head. Nevertheless there are a number of
pursuits which clearly have special intrinsic dangers, like the possibility of drowning, falling from a height, being pierced by an arrow
or bullet, or freezing to death. The main thing to do here is to be
sure that the local education authority knows exactly what is planned. Normally they will not smile upon any venture which does
not have a sound legal foundation, and in any event I should hope
it can be taken for granted that no teacher would supervise any
dangerous activity unless he felt *and could show* that he was fully
qualified to do so. A recent tragic accident in the Scottish High-
lands has shown us that even experienced teachers can run into
difficulties and it is always best to err on the side of caution.

Late Home From School

What about the legal aspects of children making their way home
after an out-of-school activity? There are a number of situations
in which at least some thought ought to be given to this. Firstly
there is the question of children, particularly young ones, going
home in the dark after having stayed on at school for a club meeting of some sort. Presumably the crossing wardens are there for a
purpose, so what are the legal implications of sending children off
home unaccompanied after the lollipop operators have gone off
duty? Any teacher who is in this position or who is about to start
an activity where it happens should not fail to seek some guidance
on the point. It might well be thought necessary, for instance, to
obtain written permission from the parents of those children who
wish to stay on after school.

Then there is the very common situation which arises when a

day trip arrives back at school at a late hour (there can be varying definitions of "late", depending upon the particular circumstances and the age of the children involved). Do we just say goodbye to the children and head purposefully for home ourselves? Or is there an obligation on us to see that the youngsters arrive home safely? It pays to be safe. I always play this one by ear. Some children are met by parents with cars and it is often possible to fix some of the others up with lifts with their friends. If it is really late and there are small children with a fair way to go, then you will probably have to take them home yourself for your own peace of mind. And as you are driving along with a car stuffed full of youngsters, it will be worth reflecting on whether your private car insurance covers you for this sort of thing.

Another thing that can happen is that boys or girls are expected to make their own way home after an away sports fixture, especially if it takes place in the local area. Their age has some bearing on this as in every other situation, but thinking in terms of what a reasonable parent would do, which is what guides most of the principles of teacher responsibility, I would consider that even in the case of the oldest children they should at least be closely questioned as to their ability to find their way home and whether they have enough money.

There are no quick answers to any of these questions of supervision — every case is likely to be different. What is important though is that the teacher who has charge of pupils out of school time or out of the building should remember to think about the legal responsibilities which are placed upon him, to the extent of finding out as far as possible what they are. Too many teachers leave things to chance. Of course, they get away with it much of the time, but their action is fool-hardy especially when it is realized that the demands of the law are actually reasonable and sensible, and on the whole just as easy to comply with as not.

Public Performances

Besides the question of supervision, the other major area of out-of-school activities which might bring a teacher into contact with the law is in connection with the mounting of musical, dramatic or other such performances. To start with it is common to find teachers ignoring the fact that any hall which is used for a public performance should have a licence for the occasion, issued by the local authority. The method of issuing these differs from place to place, so the council office should be contacted in good time for advice. This licence is no formality, and there will doubtless be a visit from a fire officer who will want to see that the exits comply with the law and that there is no fire risk on stage. I have myself seen a fireman hold his cigarette lighter to scenery to see if it was inflammable, so it is clearly necessary to take this into account when planning a production.

Copyright and Performing Rights

Remember the copyright and performing right laws. You cannot photographically reproduce or duplicate pieces of music willy nilly, for instance. It sometimes happens that a musician is invited to conduct or adjudicate at a festival, and turns up to find choirs using photographic copies of his own work. Teachers who will do this are daft enough for anything, and I would tremble if they were teaching my kids.

The way to keep on the right side of the copyright law is to make sure that proper published copies of music or plays and so on are always bought in sufficient quantity. There are some loopholes which allow for things like free reproduction on exam papers or on blackboards in classroom work, but the intention of the law is that there should be no avoidance of the necessity for buying copies, and there is really no reason why the law should not be kept.

The same is true of the performance of a copyright play. Royalties are payable on any performance of a copyright play which is open to the public — and that means parents, even if only one comes.

Advice about payment of fees for performing music as opposed to just buying it should be obtained from the Performing Right Society Ltd., 29 Berners Street, London, W1P 4AA.

And while you are about it, think carefully about such things as the casual use of records or illegal taped copies of records as incidental or interval music at public performances.

It is true that there is wholesale flouting of the law in the field of copyright and performing rights, perhaps more so in the case of the latter than of the former. I have even heard a BBC local radio official say that he "never worried" about performing rights. The point is, of course, that it is from the collection of royalties that composers and other creative artists are paid, and there is no reason why teachers, who have a positive duty towards the encouragement of the creative arts and thus an interest in the just treatment of the artist, should be party to robbery, which is what illegal reproduction and performance is.